The Spirituality of Black Preaching

by

Lewis Brogdon

Seymour Press
Bowie, MD

Copyright Seymour Press, 2016

ISBN-10:1-938373-08-1:

ISBN-13: 978-1-938373-08-4

All Scripture is from the KJV Bible unless otherwise noted.

Table of Contents

Introduction 1

Chapter One
Has Black Preaching Become a Form of Entertainment? 8

Chapter Two:
The Spirituality of Black Church Preaching 28

Chapter Three: The Two Challenges for Contemporary
    Preachers 60

Chapter Four:
The Preacher as Worshipper 76

Chapter Five:
Dealing with Opposition and Disillusionment in Ministry 100

Chapter Six:
Bishops in the Black Church: New Boundaries in Black Church
    Spirituality and Polity 114

Chapter Seven:
Pushing the Boundaries of Spirituality beyond the Four Walls of
    the Church 132

Dedication

I dedicate this book to young preachers. You will lead the church for years to come and I hope that some of what is taught here will equip you for the task ahead. I pray that God will lead you and bless the work of your hands as you preach the glorious gospel of Jesus Christ. Amen. I hope you will remember that the genius and power of black preaching is not in how you preach but what you preach and why you preach in the first place. It is not style but rather substance that you should be concerned with and should ground your preaching for years to come.

Introduction

Why Am I Writing a Book on Preaching?

I am sure that a few of my colleagues in the field of academic teaching will wonder why I am writing a book on preaching when my area of expertise is biblical studies and African American religion. My reply to them will be threefold. I am a pastor and ordained minister of twenty-three years and this has afforded me a wealth of experience to draw from in writing a book like this. I am a son of two preachers and have been raised around preachers. I have learned invaluable lessons about preaching, ministry, and Christian spirituality from them. Much of what is discussed here is a product of these great preachers. My second reply will be to push back on this whole notion of disciplines as if they are not related. I have taught preachers the writings of the New Testament and how to exegete texts in the New Testament for years. My pedagogy has always crossed the disciplines of biblical studies and homiletics, primarily because I have always been a practitioner myself. I draw on theology and history as well because careful and effective exegesis and preaching requires knowledge and skills in these disciplines. I see my task as helping students to effectively integrate these in ways that deepen sermons, stimulates faith in the context of worship, and strengthen churches as they seek to give witness to the gospel of Jesus Christ. My final response would be to discuss the wide gap I have encountered in my work in the academy and the church. I have worked in theological education at the graduate and undergraduate levels for ten years. Recruiting, teaching, and mentoring students in seminaries and a university department of religion provides limited exposure to current and future ministers. In my travels and years of preaching in churches across the country, I have found that there are hundreds and thousands of ministers who will never attend seminary or a university. Yet they will be preaching in churches and pastoring churches. They will touch hundreds and thousands of lives with no contact with us in theological education. Theological educators need to find a variety of ways to influence and teach leaders who will never sit in our classrooms. I am attempting to do this.

But the deeper reason for writing this book comes from my understanding of the nature of God's call. I grew up in the Pentecostal church tradition and Pentecostals believe God speaks to people and leads them to do specific things to advance the kingdom of God. We often refer to this as the unction of the Holy Spirit. The Spirit will stir in the deepest places of the soul and spirit until there is clarity of purpose and a willingness to step out in faith to fulfill the task. For years, God has been dealing with me about preaching. What this means is that God has troubled my spirit to address troubled areas in the church as it relates to preaching. God has done more than alert me to problems. He has spent years teaching me things in the scriptures and through my work as a scholar of the Bible and the Black Church that can address some of these areas. So I wrote because God called me to this task, knowing I am not a trained homiletics scholar. I do not pretend to be one. I am an experienced pastor, minister, biblical and religious scholar. And I write in the fullness of who I am, not who I am not. In my growing understanding of God's call, I have come to understand that when God reveals things to people he has called, he is doing so for a reason. The few times God has pointed out faults in the practices of the church to me, it has been to call me to do something to address it. This book is one of those occasions.

For years, I have witnessed African American churches drawing on younger preachers to lead churches and do the work of ministry. While it is commendable that young men and women are so willing to enter the ministry at an early age, the reality is that too many are doing so with little to no training in ministry. They are novices. They are very gifted. They are willing and available but they are not ready for the rigors of a life of ministry in times like this. One of the reasons rates of burnout, misconduct and clergy suicide are so high are because the churches are calling people to lead who are not prepared. In fact, this is my story. I entered ministry at the age of nineteen. I was very gifted but was not prepared. I did not have a single class in ministry, preaching, pastoral counseling, theology, or Bible before I was pastoring a church. I made so many mistakes that could have easily been avoided if I was trained and prepared to be a minister instead of figuring out how to be a minister on the job. There are deeper issues my narrative and many others raises that cannot be addressed here. For example, younger gifted ministers deal with professional jealousy from older clergy who sometimes leave younger ministers on their own so they can make mistakes. These mistakes are meant to reinforce the value of more experienced ministers. (Think job security). Ministry is often like the animal kingdom where younger lions are left to survive on their own. Some young preachers are placed in churches and have to figure out how to preach, what to preach, and how to handle ministry on their own. "God will lead you" is what they are told but oftentimes it does not always work out. Such practices set ministers up for mistakes, exposes congregations to harm, and discredits the integrity of ministers. There is more to this issue but I want my readers to understand this and why it is problematic. So I purposely wrote this book for younger preachers with hopes that it will find its way into their personal libraries and studies.

    In the pages of this book they will be invited to think critically and theologically about contemporary black preaching and ministry. They will be challenged to draw from the deep well of Christian spirituality to strengthen and refresh them in the lifelong call to the preaching ministry. The book will not replace the excellent textbooks on preaching that I hope they will read in college and seminary but I hope that after reading it, some will decide to pursue theological training. More importantly, I hope that this book will be instrumental in a larger work God is up to in the earth. I believe God wants to deepen our relationship with him. There is too much nominalism in our churches and a cultural brand of faith that is disconnected from the God who calls us to him in the person and work of Jesus Christ. This has happened on our watch – "ours" as in those of us who have been preaching in and leading churches for the past few decades. I have seen this in my context among the predominantly African American churches that I attend and serve. There is a preoccupation with style and less care for spiritual substance among younger ministers. It is troubling. But the problem is more widespread. It touches Protestant churches of all kind. We have not been drinking deeply enough from the wells of the Spirit and drawing on the Spirit in the work of ministry. I feel God is calling us back to this and I am hopeful that change will unfold and manifest in the decades to come.

In the following pages, I provide seven "seemingly" disconnected essays on preaching that actually form a core upon which my theology of Black Church preaching is based. I discuss the phenomenon of entertainment preaching in chapter one. I analyze the constituent elements of Black Church preaching in chapter two. The third chapter explores the role of worship in the preaching moment and why worship is important for preachers. The remaining four chapters examines issues such as the debate over the importance of teaching or preaching in black churches, opposition and disillusionment in ministry, the increasing number of bishops in black churches, and the social role of the church. These essays will discuss and frame responses to these issues by drawing on aspects of Christian spirituality. I seek to demonstrate how a robust and deep spirituality can help preachers and preaching to respond to challenges in contemporary times. I do not attempt to provide some definitive answer or solution to what ails modern preaching. Instead, I encourage young preachers to think spiritually about preaching and ministry and by doing this, they can faithfully address issues and engage in a life of effective ministry.

The last point I want to make about this book is to say that you don't have to be a Black Church pastor, minister or congregational leader to read this book. I have been reading books about theology, history, and preaching for years written by white scholars and ministers working in predominantly white churches. Their knowledge and wisdom are a product of working in these contexts. Minorities know that their suggestions are informed by a cultural context that is different from theirs yet they read them for what is applicable. I hope non-blacks readers will extend me and other minority scholars and ministers the same courtesy. Theological education is more diverse today than in years past. We teach and write books for the church with hopes of guiding the church in the important work of ministry. So why put "Black Church" preaching in the title? I believe that it is a good practice to be honest about the context from which you speak. People are a product of their cultural and historical context and speak as people in context. So this book is a product of people, movements, debates and questions among predominantly African American churches. Unlike preaching and theological books that attempt to speak to church while assuming their context is normative for everyone, this books names its context and uses it to invite others to enter the conversation and find ways to connect and utilize this book in non-black church contexts. By naming one's context and tradition, it helps readers to highlight important differences because people's cultural traditions differ. It invites readers to recognize the need more learning about particular issues, areas where greater clarification is needed and where further reflection could benefit others doing similar work. This book is not just for African American Christians. It is written in service to the church that together we may preach the good news of Jesus in the distinctiveness of various cultures and individual personalities. You will find something here to challenge and help you in this work.

Chapter One

Has Black Preaching Become a Form of Entertainment?

Black preachers and black preaching are a cultural phenomenon, drawing the interest, curiosity, inspiration, and admiration of many Americans. The American religious imagination is influenced by Dr. Martin Luther King, Jr. standing behind a pulpit and speaking to America. It is influenced by the voice of the late Rev. C. L. Franklin, by contemporary tele-evangelists such as Fred Price, Creflo Dollar, and T. D. Jakes, who was named the next Billy Graham by *Time* magazine in September 2001. Black comedians like Cedric the Entertainer and many others love mimicking black preachers. Black preachers are often included in movies portraying the African American community like *The Preacher's Wife* and *Madea Goes to Jail*. These preachers are often portrayed as charismatic, colorful, morally ambiguous, compassionate, gifted orators, and leaders. It has become commonplace to see black preacher's as a part of the fabric of this country.

Black preachers have become so prominent that many have become celebrities. They are as popular as major actors and more influential. The popular television shows *Preachers of L. A.* and *Preachers of Detroit* are recent examples of the superstardom some black preachers have reached. Scholars are also interested in black preachers and black preaching, particularly African American scholars who work in the field of homiletics (preaching). These scholars study the history of black preaching that goes back to the days of slavery and the unique way blacks interpreted Scripture to give meaning to their lives. They examine distinct practices like call and response and rhythmic cadences that sometimes lead to the hum or hooping. More importantly, they interrogate the content of black preaching to insure that it is speaking a word of hope, strength, and justice to the people of God and the world. Black preaching and preachers are getting a lot of attention.

      However, there is a danger with the preoccupation of black preaching, namely the focus on the art of black preaching and the neglect of the heart of black preaching. American culture and sadly even many black churches are more preoccupied with replicating the cadences, rhythms, and sounds of a black preacher rather than the heart. I especially see this with the cadre of younger black preachers coming up in the ranks of church leadership. I have been working with young preachers for the past decade and I am so thankful for their sense of call, their dedication to the church, and their willingness to take on leadership roles at an early age. But some of what I see is concerning. I see preachers who pay more attention to homiletical style and practices that sharpen the entertainment component of preaching. They study and practice the performance of preaching but give scarce attention to the spirituality of preaching. This is endemic of a deeper problem with black preaching that I believe the church must take on in the next two decades. I say this because I believe the next two decades are critically important for the future of black preaching and black preachers. Let me explain how I came to this conclusion.

Entertainment Preaching?

About seven years ago, the prominent theologian and religious scholar, Dr. J. Deotis Roberts spoke at a gathering of clergy at Simmons College of Kentucky about various issues related to the contemporary Black Church.[1] His informal reflections made an indelible impression on me. Two things he said stand out in my mind. He expressed his desire to see the dynamic and enthusiastic energy of Black worship translated into energy used to work for social change in our communities.[2] This was a profound insight rooted in a deep desire

---

[1] J. Deotis Roberts is one of the religious scholars and theologians to create Black Theology movement. Roberts is as prominent a figure as James Cone and at one time was highly influential among black mainline pastors. He has written over fifteen books and more than one hundred articles and essays. I highly recommend two books.

[2] This is an old debate in the African American community. For over a century some African Americans have criticized the zeal and energy of black Christian worship as misplaced or wasted altogether. Instead of investing so much energy and time in worship services, some black leaders urged that such energy be redirected to fighting injustices like racism and poverty. I recommend reading W. E. B. DuBois, The Souls of Black Folk. Introduction and Notes by Farah Jasmine Griffin. (New York: Barnes and Noble Classics, 2003). First published in 1903; Benjamin E. Mays, The Negro's God as Reflected in His Literature (New York: Russell and Russell Publishing, 1968); Benjamin Mays and Williams Nicholson, The Negro's Church (New York: Negro Universities Press, 1969) for historical context on this debate. I also recommend Dale Andrews, Practical Theology for Black Churches (Louisville: Westminster John Knox, 2002) and Raphael Warnock, The Divided Mind of the Black Church (New York: New York University Press, 2013) to explore the contemporary features of this debate. Liberation and

for a greater connection between religious zeal within the four walls of the church and religious action beyond the four walls of the church. But his comment that concerned me greatly was that many of the preaching conferences around the country have become preaching competitions. Black churches hold conferences all the time so this is a statement not to be taken lightly. His assessment of black preaching became the springboard for this study. I was deeply disturbed by this assessment not because of what he said but at the possibility it was true. Has Black preaching devolved into a form of entertainment? If so, how can we assess this unfortunate trend in our churches and how can the word of God bring correction and insight into the true nature of preaching.[3] The purpose of this study is not to point fingers but to shed new light by asking critical questions. I love the Black Church tradition but it does not mean I cannot take a critical eye and correct the areas where there is error. My criticism is rooted in a deep love for churches and pastors who have formed and nourished me in faith.

A good place to begin is to confess that it is possible to corrupt or misuse the sacred. Preaching the gospel is very sacred but that does

---

Reconciliation: A Black Theology (Philadelphia: Westminster, 1971), and *Bonhoeffer and King: Speaking Truth to Power* (Louisville: Westminster John Knox, 2005).

[3] In order to understand the distinct features of this debate, it is important to situate the debate within the practices and traditions of the Black Church. Black churches in America have unique dynamic practices and traditions of preaching and worship. For example, there is a history of call and response style of preaching that goes back to the eighteen hundreds. This style of preaching is communal, participatory, and dynamic. It is a style of preaching that also lends itself to misuse and abuse if not properly practiced. I recommend reading Evans E. Crawford, *The Hum* (Nashville: Abingdon Press, 1995) for a brief history of this practice.

not mean it cannot be abused by those called to the task. Anyone who steps up to the sacred desk and opens the Holy Scripture always walks the fine line between the holy and profane. Preaching models many paradoxes of incarnation- of the holy being entangled with what is unholy, namely humanity, and so challenges anyone aspiring to preach to walk the line carefully lest the preaching moment become contaminated with the profane instead of the holy. This struggle for balance is one reason preachers sing a hymn of preparation or offer a prayer of consecration to invoke the presence of the holy and to also submit themselves to the holy to be used by God before they preach.

    The next step in this exploration is to confess that I've seen preaching abused and misused in my time as a pastor. You may disagree with Dr. Roberts' assessment but I am sure if you've spent enough time in the Black Church you have seen a preacher or two or three "show off" or go overboard trying to impress the people with, most often his, or her rhetorical and intellectual skill. In some cases, the showing off was inadvertent while other times it was grossly blatant. However, the problem Dr. Roberts identified is more serious than the occasional show off. He proposed that preaching in church conferences has become an art form, a form of entertainment that is put on display and judged by the masses. In this sense, if the crowd likes the performance and the art form they respond with adulation and enthusiasm. As the conference progresses, so does the pressure to move the crowd or should I say impress the crowd and woe to the preacher who cannot entertain or adequately compete in the preaching arena. He or she is actually viewed in a pejorative manner as one who "cannot preach." I have heard other preachers talk about a guest preacher who "died" or "flopped" at a big conference because they could not "do it" or "cut it." The implication here is clear. They could not meet the entertainment standard.

When this happens, it validates his charge that Black preaching has devolved into a form of entertainment because a person's worth as a preacher is tied to how they perform rather than their fidelity to Scripture and the transforming gospel of Jesus Christ. This means that that the sacred nature of preaching is being undermined by the competitive impulse. And worse yet, it means that in the broader context, worship services are not places where real worship of God is happening because worship is fundamentally about devaluing human worth and wisdom and magnifying the God of all creation. This charge has significant implications for our churches.

There is something wrong with this picture. The truth is, there are conferences where thousands come to be entertained. I have attended the Hampton Ministers Conference for the past eight years. Some of the best preachers in the world preach at this conference that is attended by thousands. And sadly, in many preaching circles, conference preachers are evaluated not on the content of their preaching but instead on the entertainment value. Did he or she "kill it" or "wreck it" or did they have the crowds worked up into a "frenzy?" This is the substance of evaluations among preachers, not in depth discussions about biblical texts that were preached on or theological concepts introduced that may deepen our preaching. In some respects, black preaching has lost its way because I believe there is so much more to the black preaching tradition than entertaining large crowds of people with rhetoric, intelligence, and charisma.

Preaching in the Contemporary Black Church

In order to adequately address this issue we have to get inside of some of the dynamics that led to preaching becoming focused on entertainment. We will begin with a dynamic that is distinctly ecclesial in nature before moving to more secular influences. The first issue is the preponderance of church conferences. Both denominational and nondenominational churches in America seem to be in love with the notion of putting on annual church conferences. These conferences feature workshops, worship, and preachers all under a conference theme that has relevance for the participants and host church, ministry, or judicatory. For Christians with denominational experience, these conferences have replaced revivals that were a staple of the church for decades.

Today, conferences draw large crowds of people together many times in large sanctuaries or civic centers. Why is this significant? In the black context the ability to organize, plan, and successfully conduct conferences of this magnitude represents progress from very humble beginnings. Black Christians have in many respects gone from storefronts and used sanctuaries to state of the art facilities. So naturally there is a great sense of godly pride and accomplishment for what God has done. However, if godly pride goes unchecked it has the potential to change into sinful pride that is ungodly and unwholesome.

It is godly pride when the glory goes and stays with God while it is ungodly when we begin to give ourselves glory and think more highly of ourselves than we ought to. One thing that Scripture reinforces over and over again is that it is difficult to handle godly success. The story of Israel as an enslaved people to a mighty nation bears this lesson out. It is also evident through the individual persons that God providentially called and blessed as they obeyed him. For example, King David started from humble beginnings as a shepherd boy. God anointed him to be king of Israel and greatly blessed him. But once he was king, he struggled to handle the success. He took Bathsheba, the wife of Uriah, and had him killed to cover the fact that he raped and impregnated her (2 Sam 11). He spent years with turmoil in his house because of his disobedience and wayward heart (2 Samuel 12-1 Kgs 1). The same was true for his son Solomon, who God blessed with great wealth and wisdom. He started out with such promise but his heart was turned away from the Lord and chased after other gods (1 Kgs 11:1-8).

This is particularly relevant for the Black Church. Not in all, but in some respects, we have made significant progress and the temptation is to think that "my power and my might have gotten me this wealth" (see Deuteronomy 8:17). How does this influence the entertainment impetus in the Black Church? That is the question. When we forget that God has brought us a mighty long way and we begin to glory in the success that he has given us, the temptation in preaching is to bask in the glory of success and to draw attention away from God and to yourself by using your God-given gift to preach. Such basking is only possible when God has given his blessing both in the forms of communal progress and individual gifting for ministry. Instead of carefully walking in God's light, the temptation is to use that light to draw attention to self.

The second issue that influences this is the growth of television ministries and preachers. Preaching has been significantly changed by the advent of the lights, camera, and action of popular media. Initially many in the church saw television as a medium for the advancement of the gospel. In other words, TV gives the church a larger platform to get the word out about Jesus.[4] Now I admit this sounds credible. But something changed. Instead of using television as a conduit for the proclamation of the gospel, ministries, churches, and preachers began using it as a means to promote themselves. Anyone watching TV ministries knows that very little actually preaches Christ. If one were to watch a telecast, they would hear about almost everything but Jesus and him crucified.

Why did this happen? In America the church has become heavily influenced by what James Hudnut Beumler termed

---

[4] For an insightful study of the influence of tele-evangelism on African Americans read Jonathan Walton, Watch This (New York: New York University Press, 2009).

"entrepreneurial Protestantism."[5] This refers to the way ministries and churches have become market driven and market savvy in what has become a religious market place.[6] Church life and its varied ministries have become commodified and infused with the business of marketing and economics. In order to gain influence and a hearing with today's religious consumers, churches have created sophisticated economic and marketing mechanisms. One of the fundamental rules of economics is supply and demand. The better equipped one is to meet demand with supply the more profitable they will become.

    Why is this important? The advent and growth of television ministries provided market driven ministries with an opportunity compete in the religious and many times secular market. It also gave the really creative preachers opportunities to develop their own market niche. One lesson learned from their secular counterparts was the importance of advertising. How can ministries meet demand unless people know they have the goods that you need? As a result, television became the tool to promote ministry products instead of being a tool for the advancement of the gospel. Another fundamental rule of economics is to advertise a good to superior product. Why? Because there is always market competition, even in the religious sector. When

---

    [5] James Hudnut Beumler, *In Pursuit of the Almighty's Dollar: A History of Money and American Protestantism* (Chapel Hill: University of North Carolina Press, 2007), 212.

    [6] If you are interested in an Evangelical appraisal of the influence of marketing practices and philosophies on American churches read Gary Gilley, *This Little Church Went to the Market* (Evangelical Publishing Books, 1995) and Barry Taylor, *Entertainment Theology* (Grand Rapids: Baker Academic, 2008).

preachers get in front of the camera they have to impress those who are in the market for either ministry products like books, teaching cds and dvds, upcoming conferences with popular guest speakers, or those looking for a church to join. Hence the impetus to entertain, to become a religious salesman, and cheerleader meant to arouse the passions for consumerism that comes in many different forms. Once the system functions to perpetuate these kinds of ministries, even newer ministries have to inevitably compete to keep up. The singing, exhortation, and preaching has to connect in some respect with the competitive or entertainment impetus if it is to remain relevant and viable. This trend has had a significant impact on preaching and preachers. It has required them to integrate aspects of performance into the homiletical trade.

    The third dynamic behind this unfortunate trend is the tendency of black churches to be centered around the preacher, pastor, and or bishop. Now I know that there is going to be some disagreements on this point but anyone knowledgeable about the history of the Black Church understands the importance and the central nature that the preacher has in the church. More so than other Christian traditions, the black preacher enjoys a place of prominence and great influence over the lives of its parishioners. And not only from a historical standpoint, but my experience as a pastor in the Black Church and my friends who are pastors in black churches can say "amen" to what I am saying. Your objection can be rooted in a critique that this ought not to be. I am more than willing to have that conversation. But I am largely convinced that in many, not all, black churches the preacher is the central figure and exercises significant influence.

If a church has a competent, caring, and charismatic black pastor chances are he or she will exercise great influence. When thinking about black pastors of mega-churches they are almost given celebrity status. In fact, it could be argued that they are religious icons in the black community. From the slave preacher to the mega-church pastor, the central role they occupy opens them up to the entertainment impetus. Jesus was careful when the crowds gathered around. He would challenge them when he sensed they were glory seeking and looking for more miracles and signs.

From the wilderness temptation to successful campaigns throughout Galilee he constantly refused the false adulation of the crowds and never placated to their desire to be entertained. In fact, Jesus would sometimes respond with harsh challenges and charges to test the validity of their commitment to the kingdom. It takes a really big person to do that. Black preaching has suffered because on too many occasions there are preachers who relish the limelight and give the crowds what they want so they can keep them coming back. Instead of turning away insincere and uncommitted followers, some of today's black preachers go out of their way to please them for one day a week.

The fourth and final dynamic behind the shift toward entertainment in preaching is the portrayal of black preachers in television and movies. This is by no means a flattering part of the essay but it is a dose of truth that should challenge all black preachers to evaluate what we do and the message we send to society. Black preaching and black preachers have become the laughing stock of many television shows and movies. One does not have to wait too long before an actor or actress comes parading in front of the camera pretending to be a preacher. There are even quite a few black comedians who mimic black preachers so convincingly that the crowds can hardly stand it. The sad truth is that their depiction is sometimes accurate. Again the question is, why? Could it be possible that actors are so good at mocking black preaching and preachers because much of what they see looks like entertainment?

    Let me make some important caveats here. First of all, I do not agree that all black preachers fit the common stereotype of black emotionally charged preaching. Black preaching is by no means monolithic. Secondly, I am greatly concerned about the entertainment executives who decide to repeatedly send pejorative messages about black preachers. It has a negative influence on people's perceptions of black preachers. Finally, the mocking of black preaching is a much larger critique of the perception of the Black Church as a place where people come to carry on and have a good time. The perception is the emotionalism evident in the singing and the call and response form of preaching that is devoid of spiritual substance or social relevance. This unfortunate perception is unfounded in some respects while accurate in others. Black preachers should be aware of the growing perception that they are becoming entertainers and not agents of change. One should remember how television is used to promote preacher's ministries. The exposure is a two-edged sword because it provides wider exposure and wider criticism. Now that we have unpacked the various dynamics at work here let us look at some solutions.

Lessons on Preaching from the Church at Corinth

Ironically this is not a new problem in the church. In fact, one of, if not, the most troubled congregations in the New Testament had a form of this kind of problem- the church at Corinth.[7] Paul heard that there were divisions in the church (I Cor 1:10-17). Corinthian believers began quarreling and dividing over their favorite preachers: Paul, Apollos, and Cephas. A helpful aside, Apollos, we are told in Acts 18:24 was mighty in speech which is possibly an indicator that he was trained in Greek rhetoric and philosophy. It is clear from Paul's comments in the first three chapters that the Corinthians were enamored with worldly wisdom (Greek *sophia*) and thus began to prefer Apollos over Paul and maybe even to pit them against each other among themselves. Sound familiar? In these first three chapters Paul makes two compelling arguments: he downplays the significance of worldly wisdom with his meditation on the foolishness of preaching in I Corinthians Sa1:18-31, and he argues that instead of being in

---

[7] Two incredibly good commentaries on this Pauline letter are Gordon Fee, *The First Epistle to the Corinthians*, New International Commentary on the New Testament (Grand Rapids: Eerdmans Publishing, 1987) and C. K. Barrett, *The First Epistle to the Corinthians*, Black's New Testament Commentary (Peabody MA: Hendricksen, 1993).

competition with one another, God uses one preacher to plant and another to water but ultimately increase, blessing, and growth comes only from God in 3:1-9.

Central to Paul's reasoning is the motif of divine reversal, a motif that is commonly used in the New Testament. Jesus used role reversal often by saying that the last shall be first or by using outcasts as key figures in the kingdom of God i.e. the Samaritan man in Luke 10 or poor Lazarus in Luke 16. Paul uses this same principle in 1:20-31 to reinforce how foolish it is to glory in human wisdom. In this passage God takes human wisdom and mocks it by using the foolishness of preaching. Instead of impressing would be converts, God uses a practice that would be repulsive (folly to Gentiles v. 23) to be the conduit of eternal salvation. In fact, God rejects human wisdom because it does not lead to saving faith nor display humility or self-denial, a characteristic of Jesus Christ and anyone who would follow him. In verses 28-29, Paul says, "God chose what is low and despised in the world, even things that are not, to bring to nothing things that are, so that no human being might boast in the presence of God."

So by inadvertently placing their allegiance with human wisdom, the Corinthians demonstrated a profound sense of foolishness that stood at odds with God's work in the world. That is why Paul did not come to Corinth trying to impress them with human wisdom (2:1-5). In humility and weakness, he preached Christ and the works that were done through him were because of God using him. So even here you see the symmetry of his argument in 1:18-31, the foolishness and wisdom of God's plan. In 2:1-5, God uses the weak and lowly to demonstrate his mighty power, and 3:1-9, God uses different vessels to bring blessing to the church. What a poignant lesson this has for the Black Church.

Like the church at Corinth, we too are impressed with human wisdom and demonstrations of human eloquence- human *sophia*. Black preaching possibly more so than preaching in other traditions, has the potential to impress its followers. Hearing a black preacher read, interpret, and expound on the significance of the biblical text for our contemporary context is a powerful experience. The rhetorical power and hypnotizing cadence of the skilled preacher can hoodwink spiritually immature congregants into thinking that the preacher is more than he or she appears.

When God's hand is upon the preacher and the presence of God is moving, people can look at them as larger than life figures; when in all actuality they are only vessels of God. The Corinthians had taken what God had given them and exalted it above measure, when in fact God chose the foolishness of preaching as the ultimate expression of divine power and wisdom. Again, through the foolishness of preaching Christ reveals the power and wisdom of God, not human power or wisdom. Therefore, as it relates to black preaching, Paul is challenging the Black Church to redirect its attention and adoration back to God and not the human representative called to speak for God. In addition, we must reject the tendency to appear strong or wise from worldly standards.

Paul came to Corinth not to impress the people but actually came in weakness. The world encourages us to impress people and to draw attention to ourselves. With a long history of powerful preaching, the tendency to impress people must be kept in check. The gospel calls for us to reject that instinct because it does not reveal the power and wisdom of God. Remember the words of Jesus in Matthew that when we practice our righteousness before people the only reward we receive is their temporary acclaim (6:1-4).

Faithful Black Preaching

For some reason, people have mistaken the true genius of black preaching. Black preaching is what it is because of the role of the faithful black preacher to the black experience, an experience rooted in fighting evils such as centuries of slavery and racism.[8] Black preaching is at its best when it helps oppressed and marginalized people make sense of the vicissitudes of daily life and find meaning and hope to forge ahead in faith. Slaves in the late 1700s and throughout 1800s did not need the preacher to entertain them. They needed someone who could speak a word of hope and empowerment as they struggled for survival.[9]

---

[8] See Henry Mitchell, *Black Preaching* (Nashville: Abingdon Press, 1990) for a helpful two-chapter study of the history of black preaching.

[9] I recommend doing a little study of slave preachers. Two sources to get you started are Albert Raboteau, *Slave Religion* (New York: Oxford University Press, 2001) and an essay written by Eugene Genovese entitled, "Black Plantation Preachers in the Slave South." Paul Finkelman, *Religion and Slavery* (New York: Garland Publishing, 1987).

I often wonder what it must have been like to pastor and preach to enslaved Africans. Spending years trying to instill a sense of meaning and hope amidst meaningless and hopeless conditions. If I could talk to any person from a different historical era, not counting Jesus Christ who is first on my list, I would want to talk with a slave preacher. How did you preach when white slaveholders tried to keep the gospel from blacks or when they tried to domesticate the gospel to justify slavery? How do you preach without a Bible, without a building called a church, or to intelligent people who were illiterate? These are a few questions I would pose to them. I am utterly amazed at the ways God's blessed these people and the first African churches in America because of their dedication and gifts for preaching good news.

This was undoubtedly a formidable task that required the best energies, intellect, compassion, and spirit of the preacher. I'm not the only one who has reflected on the formidable task and importance of the black preacher. Howard Thurman's lectures on the Negro Spirituals delivered at Harvard University approached the subject by first highlighting the importance of the work of the preacher in creating conditions where spirituals can flourish. Before such spirituals as *Sometimes I Feel like a Motherless Child, Nobody Knows the Trouble I've Seen, Swing Low Sweet Chariot*, and *The Gospel Train*, writers were instructed and inspired by black preachers, a point often missed in studies of the Spirituals. Thurman began with the Negro preacher saying the following:

> The antebellum Negro preacher was the greatest single factor in determining the spiritual destiny of the slave community…you are created in God's image. You are not niggers; you are God's children…It is out of this sense of being a child of God that the genius of the religious folk song is born…many weary, spiritually and physically exhausted slaves found new strength and power gushing up into all the reaches of their personalities, inspired by the words that fell from this man's lips. He had discovered that which religion insists is the ultimate truth about human life and destiny. It is the supreme validation of the human spirit. He who knows this is able to transcend the vicissitudes of life, however terrifying, and look out on the world with quiet eyes. It is out of this sense of being a child of God that the genius of the folk songs is born.[10]

In particular, the preacher's affirmation to slaves that they were children of God represents one of the core functions of the Black Preacher which was to provide a different center of meaning than being exploited chattel and a source of hope than a God who predestines blacks to a life of servitude. Black preachers gave their people a sense of "somebodiness."

    It is striking to consider the significance of preachers and their role in helping African Americans transcend to varying degrees the

---

[10] Howard Thurman, *Deep River: The Negro Spiritual Speaks of Life and Death* (Friends United Press, 1975), 12.

horrors of slavery. This is the tradition of preaching that we inherited from our ancestors and the tradition we strive to honor every time God gives us the opportunity to preach. Contemporary black preachers should strive to honor this tradition of preaching because it continues to be a "significant factor in determining the destiny of the African American community."

As our community confronts the stark realities and inequities linked to 246 years of legalized slavery, 103 years of Jim and Jane Crow Segregation, and 45 years of visible and invisible forms of discrimination, the work of serious black preachers and pastors is as important as it was during the era of slavery. Black Americans rank at the top in crime, murders, drug abuse, unemployment, incarceration, poverty, education, divorce, HIV/AIDS and worse yet a rate of suicide that has been steadily increasing for years. Our community is on the fast track to ruin and is in need of pastors who are faithful to the formidable tasks of preaching and ministering to African American people. Howard Thurman summed up what I believe is the true genius of black preaching. (1) building up God's people, (2) providing encouragement to the downtrodden, and (3) inspiring people to work for change and social uplift. If more of this kind of preaching was going on in conferences imagine what we could do. Instead of having a good time, imagine if Black preaching encouraged the weak and inspired us all to make a difference in the world.

Chapter Two

The Spirituality of Preaching

When thinking about the awesome task of preaching it is critically important to attend to the spirituality of the preacher as much as the skills, study, and preparation that make for good preaching. In fact, one of the primary reasons or motivating factors behind this booklet is the dearth in emphasizing the spirituality of preaching and particularly the spirituality of the preacher. The church desperately needs two things for effective ministry- skilled pastors and truly spiritual pastors.

The problem is that both are emphasized separately depending on the church tradition. Let me explain. Some churches require theological training for ministry. Men and women who feel called to the ministry have to attend seminary or a university divinity school and study subjects like Hebrew, Greek, exegesis, theology, pastoral care and practical theology. The educational process, in addition, to the requirements for ordination take over three years. With such a heavy load of courses and ordination requirements, sometimes one's spirituality suffers and is grossly neglected.

There are even a few leaders in these churches that criticize non-theologically trained pastors and ministers. They believe all a person needs for effective ministry is to learn how to be an effective pastor. There are also churches that criticize people who attend seminary. They argue that the seminary is the place where you lose your faith and is spiritually dead. They joke about theological "cemeteries" all the time. They surmise that all one needs to be an effective pastor is the Spirit and a passion for ministry. Instead of insisting on one way to prepare ministry, imagine if both came together? If this happened, 21st century preaching could have a significant impact on the needed rejuvenation of American Protestantism, which is steadily declining in numbers and social significance.

Skilled and Trained Clergy

Today's 21st century Christian context need skilled and well-trained preachers. There was a time when uneducated ministers were commonplace in the Black Church but that time has apparently ended. The advent of the information age, characterized by free exchange of ideas and beliefs via the internet and various social media platforms, in addition to higher levels of education among many parishioners results in a need for educated pastors. Skilled pastors bring intellectual depth to the tasks of preaching, teaching, and administration. They are students of history and sociology and understand how the world works. Skilled pastors are passionate communicators and have leadership gifts. But skills are developed through training and study, which is why theological institutions are so important. The apostle Paul admonished those who desire to lead the church should attend to doctrinal matters and must study to show themselves approved to God (1 Tim 4:16; 2 Tim 2:15; Tit 1:9). This form of study is commonly referred to as theological education. In a few colleges and mostly in university divinity schools and denominational seminaries, leaders who feel called by God to go into ministry receive the necessary training to be skilled and competent in their work for God and God's people.

Let me clarify an earlier statement about the time being up for untrained clergy. One of the most important aspects of preaching is dealing with ideological matters. In other words, effective preaching has to inevitably deal with what people believe. In Romans 12:1-2, Paul encouraged the church to offer themselves as living sacrifices to God. In verse 2 he states, "And do not be conformed to this world but be ye transformed by the renewing of the mind." It is interesting that Paul connects our transformation to how we process thoughts and beliefs. The more our thinking resembles the truth of God's word and kingdom, the more our lives will begin to experience transformation.

Preaching is a vital part of this lifelong process. In preaching we help our congregants not to be conformed to the world, a largely an ideological matter for Paul. Worldliness means we follow the ideologies and belief-systems of the world. Now let's go deeper. If preaching has to inevitably deal with what people believe how one can be an effective preacher without knowing the history and development of ideas? One of the flaws or weaknesses of untrained clergy is that they are not aware of the history of ideas and movements that are germane and relevant for the way people think today. Untrained clergy do not ask where this belief came from because they have not been taught to ask such questions. Many times they naively assume that everybody thinks a certain way. As a result, some beliefs and ideas that are conformed to the world get passed on through the years because the one called by God to deal with the intersection of the ideological and doctrinal is not equipped to do so.

Trained clergy also need to be exposed to learning outside the discipline of religion. Pastors need to understand mental illness and its effects on people and families. Pastors need to understand that mental illness is not a product of demonic possession or influence. They also need to be aware of the therapists in their community who can help these people find balance and healing. Clergy today need to understand social problems such as poverty, unemployment, violence, under-educated groups of people, health disparities, and controversial issues like racism, sexism and classism. Such issues command a multi-prong approach that involves preaching, education in the congregation, education in the broader community, social advocacy and legislation, and election of better public officials.

Ministry is not about preaching sermons on Sunday. Ministry is all encompassing and includes tasks such as preaching, education, leadership, advocacy, and caring for people in need. In order to effectively carry out the duties of a minister one needs expertise, competence, acumen, skills, and a knowledge base that is broad yet has appropriate depth.

Spiritual Leaders

Today's 21st century church context also needs spiritual leaders who have a relationship with God, leaders who have saving faith in Jesus Christ, whose lives are energized by the Holy Spirit, and leaders who are connected to the church in spite of the good, bad, and the ugly in the church. Spiritual pastors are men and women with a deep and real connection to God and the people we are called to minister. Spiritual pastors read Scripture for their personal lives and for preaching and teaching. Spiritual pastors pray in faith and worship God in humility and sincerity. Spiritual pastors are attuned to human need and work to minister to it.

Yes, the church needs trained pastors but that is not all we need. On the other end of the spectrum there is a growing number of trained clergy who do not have an adequate spiritual base to enter the gospel ministry. All the skills and training in the world will not make a difference when there is such an absence in spirituality. Knowledge of Hebrew and Greek in hearts with no faith in God does not make for effective preaching.

Again let's go back to Paul's model of preaching. In Romans 1:16 he boldly claimed that the gospel is the power of God that leads to salvation. I think that today's 21st century high-tech society minimizes the efficacy of spiritual power. At the end of the day the gospel is at its core God's power at work in the world. The gospel is not based solely on human initiative, knowledge, or creativity. Paul did not set out to carry a good message inspired by human will to the world. Paul was called by God, loved by Christ, and energized by the Spirit. It was the spiritual encounter and reality that propelled him into ministry. No wonder he made such a difference.

When the spirituality of preaching is minimized we have taken the fundamental wrong approach to the task altogether because human learning and training must be grounded in a vibrant spirituality. In 1 Corinthians 2:1-5, Paul said this about preaching.

> *And I, when I came to you brothers, did not come proclaiming to you the testimony of God with lofty speech or wisdom. For I decided to know nothing among you except Jesus Christ and him crucified, And I was with you in weakness and in fear and much trembling, and my speech and my message were not in plausible words of wisdom, but in demonstration of the Spirit and of power, that your faith might not rest in the wisdom of men but in the power of God.*

The foundation of Paul's preaching ministry was the Spirit and power of God and not human wisdom. He did not rely on his rabbinic training. Yes, he utilized it but he preached in the power of God so that those who heard and believed in Christ would stand on God. True and efficacious spirituality must be rooted in an awareness of the Spirit's presence in our lives and daily fellowship with the Spirit. True spirituality comes from walking in the Spirit. Fellowship with the Spirit in prayer, study, meditation, and worship animates and energizes not only one's preaching but one's life. Indeed, this pattern seems to be consistent in the New Testament. Jesus did not enter ministry without the presence of the Spirit and Jesus did not allow his disciples to engage in ministry without the power of the Spirit. And yet churches and religious institutions send people to ministry who have not been empowered by the Spirit or sent by the Spirit.

Today's church appears to have found a different way of doing ministry. And yet as we survey the landscape of this country, it is apparent that the abundance of churches does little to stymie the onslaught of injustice, immorality, hatred, and other forms of evil inundating our world.   If the church is to recapture its relevance and efficacy in preaching and ministry, then there must be a clarion call to preachers to prepare themselves for the complex dynamics of ministry in the 21st century and a call back to what I call the spirituality of preaching. Preaching is rooted in spiritual realities that make a substantive difference in the life of the church. I believe that one life energized by the Spirit can change the world. Jesus changed the world. His mother Mary changed the world. His disciple Peter changed the world. His apostle Paul changed the world. And his disciples have been doing it for two thousand years.

Preaching in the Spirit

Preaching by its definition implies proclamation or communication with divine meaning and significance. I believe it is impossible to preach effectively without an awareness of the Spirit and the power of the Spirit. There is no such thing as preaching without

Spirit-inspired energy and guidance. Without the Spirit, it is merely public speaking. And yet preaching textbooks do not talk about the role of the Spirit in preaching. Why? They do not take the Spirit's role in preaching very seriously. The Spirit is very much at the center of the preaching task and the preacher's guide in the ministry of preaching.

In the constant shifting of ideas in the church important truths are being minimized or left out to the demise and weakening of the church. And one of those omitted spiritual truths is the need for spiritual power. The Spirit-filled church used to emphasize that the baptism of the Holy Spirit provided power for living and ministry. Today that message has fallen on tough times as pastors highlight the need for prosperity and self-fulfillment. But there is no substitute for the anointing and the power of God in a believer's life.

In fact, you know the anointing when you see it. God never intended the church to do his work in their own power. Even Jesus operated in the power of the Spirit. After his baptism the Spirit descended empowering him to minister effectively. So when Jesus preached and ministered people noticed that there was a qualitative difference in it versus the religious leaders.

> *And it came to pass when Jesus had ended these sayings the people were astonished at his doctrine: for he taught them as one having and not as the scribes (Matt 7:28-29).*

The same also holds true for preaching and singing in church. When you hear preaching or singing under the anointing it makes a substantial difference. The anointing destroys the yoke of bondage. Whereas, people who are gifted or extremely talented can preach or sing but the power of the Spirit is not at work. I have been in church where the preacher knew all the right buttons to push and all the right things to say but nothing life changing was present. But when the Word is declared in the power of the Spirit lives are changed, minds are renewed, and people are challenged to respond to the voice of God. It doesn't matter if it is preaching or teaching, when the anointing is present, lives are changed. That is what the church needs to recover. We need the power of God in the church and believers who walk in the power of the Spirit. We don't need games or gimmicks. We don't need just talented people. And the last thing the church needs is more entertainment that excites instead of changes people. It is only the power of God that can really impact a dying world.

It All Starts with Holiness

Holiness may be the most essential element to a Spirit empowered life. Holiness is a term with a lot of baggage in the church. When people hear the term holiness they often think it means moral perfection. Sadly, one of the reasons for this misunderstanding is some Christians who claim they're holy because they believe they comply with God's commands better than others. Holiness means dedication to

God, not moral perfection. In the Old Testament, the Levites were called and set apart as priests to the Lord.

This level of dedication was substantially different from the elect call of God that the rest of the tribes received. The Levites were exclusively dedicated to the Lord as priests. Certain objects in the tabernacle and later the Temple were also exclusively dedicated to the service and worship of God. The most sacred vessel in Israel was the Ark of the Covenant. When someone or something was exclusively dedicated to God it had to be treated in a holy manner. Such vessels were not treated as normal. Since the ark was the "Ark of God" you didn't treat it like any other thing. If you don't believe me, ask the person who tried to steady the ark with his hand and was struck dead. When Aaron and Miriam opposed Moses who was exclusively called and dedicated to God as the deliverer they were struck with leprosy. The implication is that when someone or something belongs to God, it is holy and therefore not to be treated as common. That is where the Old Testament understanding of holiness comes from, especially in Leviticus.

It is more important to see yourself as one who is dedicated to God and God's work instead of a person who is morally perfect. When someone or something is dedicated to God then it should be treated in a special manner. This means that your life should be characterized by high moral standards and personal integrity. You should always strive to live the life you're preaching and not do anything to bring a reproach on the ministry- cheating, lying, betraying sacred trusts, and exploiting the vulnerable. But never confuse striving to live this life with actually being morally perfect. The latter is not possible. No matter how consecrated a life you lead you will wrestle with the flesh and your own sinfulness. At times, you will fall short of the high standards you have for yourself and standards the church holds clergy to. When you do, forgive yourself, be accountable, learn from your mistakes, be gracious, and commit to moving forward.

This is why I love what the New Testament teaches about holiness. Instead of select individuals, objects, or places being made or declared holy like in the Old Testament, the blood of Jesus makes all who believe in him a holy nation (see 1 Ptr 2:9). And as such, our holiness first springs from the finished work of Christ on the cross and not our ability to comply with the commandments in the Bible. We are holy because Jesus made us holy before God with his atoning sacrifice. In the New Testament, holiness begins with Christ. I really like that because it keeps us from thinking we do things to be holy. What Christians are called to do is to pursue holiness, not to claim holiness as a moral commodity they have acquired or attained.

Follow peace with all men and holiness without which no man shall see the Lord (Heb 12:14).

Let us cleanse ourselves from all filthiness of the flesh and spirit, perfecting holiness in the fear of God (2 Cor 7:1).

These texts reinforce the importance of pursuing holiness. I like to think of holiness as dedicating oneself to God in a way that His presence, power, and gifts transform your life and enable you to effectively do His will. The life dedication does not make us sinless or perfect but it does change our habits, desires, and values in ways that make us better servants of God.

So what does holiness have to do with preaching? Holiness is important in preaching because of spiritual power. Effective preaching is animated by the presence and power of the Spirit and the preacher should be attuned to the Spirit both before and during the preaching moment. Sin, which for Christians implies willful disobedience of known commands (Jas 4:17), weakens the ways we access spiritual power. I say this because sin disrupts our fellowship with God. And when fellowship is disrupted the potency of our spiritual power in preaching diminishes. Jesus was the model. He was totally dedicated and in communion with the Father. This is one reason his preaching was so effective.

When holiness is missing in the life of a believer, the Spirit's ability to empower them in life and ministry is hindered. Paul taught churches that the Spirit can be quenched and grieved. How? Through compromise and sin, spiritual power is slowly lost until the flesh is the controlling influence in life. The Bible calls this person a carnal believer (see 1 Cor 3:1; Rom 8:1-14). When carnality is the controlling influence, spiritual power will always be missing. I know when my life is fully yielded to God in holiness my life and ministry operate on a whole new level than when worldliness and sin are present. Spiritual power flows more effectively and unhindered through a holy vessel. Do not let sin, worldliness, and compromise rob you of spiritual power. Just as God used special vessels in the Old Testament, today, dedicated Christians can be greatly used and effective in the church.

Preachers Need to Pray

There was an old saying I remember from my days in the Church of God in Christ (C.O.G.I.C.). The church mothers used to say, "Little prayer little power. No prayer no power." Why did they say this? They said this because of a strong belief in the power of prayer and how an active and effective prayer life can empower your ministry, especially the ministry of preaching. Preachers ought to be men and women of prayer. In Acts 6, Peter called ministers to serve the Grecians.

> *"But we will give ourselves continually to prayer and to the ministry of the word" (Acts 6:4).*

Peter and the other apostles did not want the daily matters of ministry to obstruct them from their primary responsibility to give themselves first to prayer and second to the ministry of the word. It is important to note the order of Acts 6:4 as it relates to ministry. Peter mentioned prayer first then preaching. This says something about the importance of prayer.

It may sound strange and be hard to believe but a lot of pastors do not pray regularly. They offer plenty of prayers in their official capacity as pastors but they do not have a personal prayer life. This has significant implications for preaching and ministry. There was a time when the disciples could not operate in the power of God and Jesus told them that there are times when fasting and prayer are needed.

> *And when he was come into the house, his disciples asked him privately, why could not we cast him out? And he said unto them, this kind can come forth by nothing, but by prayer and fasting (Mk 9:28-29).*

This incident in the life of Jesus reminds us of the above statement that I used to hear about little prayer and little power. It reflects a deep belief in prayer as one of the avenues by which spiritual power flows through the believer. It begins with the understanding that prayer is more than the time when we get to ask God for blessings. When our minds are transformed to view prayer as communion with God it becomes apparent that spiritual power is closely associated with prayer. When we commune with God we receive not only instruction from God, but the power to carry out divine instruction. When we also understand that in prayer we cast our cares on the Lord and release ourselves from anxiety about the cares of the world, prayer again becomes a source of spiritual empowerment. These are but a few reasons prayer is critical for preachers and without it they may find themselves unable to exorcize the demonic and overcome challenges in life and ministry.

Principles of Spirit-Inspired Preaching

Let me say a few words about Spirit-inspired and Spirit-led preaching by beginning with a word about preaching. I think it is important that we are honest about what preaching is in the first place. Many lift a very high standard of preaching when they use the term biblical preaching. They assume this model of preaching focuses only on the Bible and not based on human wisdom, social issues, or personal insight.

The truth is even what preachers call biblical preaching is interpretative in nature. They may call it biblical preaching but they read and explain the text or interpret its meaning for a contemporary audience. They are preaching a message that may be based on the text but their sermon is a message nonetheless. The question is what motivates and inspires the message. I believe the Spirit, not human wisdom or personal insight should guide our preaching. Our preaching should flow from a robust encounter and continual communion with the Holy Spirit that is nurtured in prayer, meditation, study, and reflection both with God and other godly men and women called to sharpen your preaching and help you live out this sacred calling.

The first principle of Spirit-inspired and Spirit-led preaching is that preaching deals with what God is saying not merely conveying biblical truths- what God said in the past. The relevance of preaching lies in the fact that it tells the people of God what God is saying about the world and life situations and not just what God said about the world and other's situations in the past. Many people today are turned off by preaching because it is overly focused on the past. What God said and did in times past must be held in balance with what God is saying and doing in the world today. Preaching requires knowledge of the biblical story and world as well as knowledge of the contemporary world and life in general.

When a preacher has knowledge of both and they are in tune with the Spirit through prayer, meditation, study, and worship they can hear the voice of the Spirit and receive messages, guidance, and instruction. The Spirit will literally teach you and give you insight that becomes the grounds for messages the Spirit has for the church. This insight will illumine the task of ministry initiatives and programs needed to bring healing, transformation, and equity to our communities. The Spirit will give you a word from the Lord, not just a Sunday sermon because nothing changes a life like a word from God. A vibrant spiritual life, coupled with knowledge, makes preaching an encounter with the active, dynamic, and powerful voice of God.

The second principle of Spirit-inspired and Spirit led preaching is that preaching must address matters of eternity, matters of faith, and matters of justice. The Spirit always deals with these critical issues. One problem in the church is that preachers tend to only deal with one or another instead of all three. Spirit filled preaching insists on calling people to decision about eternity and keeping matters of eternity before people who often ignore or refuse to consider the specter of the eternal. Where a person will spend eternity and how God's vision of eternity challenges us to live are the two most important issues for the preacher. God wills that all spend an eternity with him in fellowship and joyful worship.

> *The Lord is not slack concerning his promise as some men count slackness but is longsuffering to us-ward not willing that any should perish, but that all should come to repentance (2 Ptr 3:9).*

God has made provisions for the salvation of every person through the shed blood of Jesus Christ. However, the exercise of faith and baptism are essential to enter into this experience.

> *Go ye into all the world and preach the gospel to every creature. He that believes and is baptized shall be saved but he that believeth not shall be condemned (Mk 16:15-16).*

> *Then Peter said unto them, repent and be baptized every one of you in the name of Jesus Christ for the remission of sins, and ye shall receive the gift of the Holy Ghost (Acts 2:38).*

This exercise of faith ensures life abundantly here and eternal life to come. Now there are too many preachers who neglect the eternal component of the gospel. But they do so because they are not influenced by the Spirit. Jesus said that the Spirit will convict the world of righteousness and judgment (Jn 16:7-11). The implication is clear. The Spirit speaks a word of love and comfort, but also has something to say about sin and judgment both in this world and the world to come. The message of judgment has particular import as it relates to eternity.

Spirit-inspired and led preaching deals with matters of life. It insists on speaking a word to those dealing with difficult life circumstances. Life situations warrant a word from God. This is a different starting point. Some traditions begin the preaching task with the question of God's existence while others begin with the question of God's care. In other words, the existential question is paramount in Spirit filled preaching. God does care about the lives of his people.

Spirit filled preaching ought to be rooted in God's concern for others. The intersection between faith and doubt, bondage and deliverance strikes at the heart of this concern. God cares about the things that hold people down. God cares about the things that enslave and snare souls. God wills for all people to experience freedom and joy. As a result, through the Spirit he guides the sermon to speak to issues in a way that exposes our complicity in sin and instructs what needs to be done to experience deliverance and lasting freedom. No one is closer to the existential issues of life than the Spirit. Romans 8 instructs that the Spirit searches the heart and mind. If the Spirit knows enough about us to intercede for us in prayer, then the Spirit will also send us the messages that we need to live faithfully for God.

When people think of the work of the Holy Spirit in preaching, they often emphasize the importance of the anointing or preaching messages that are divinely inspired by God and speak directly to people's life situations. However, there is a dimension to Spirit-filled preaching that is often neglected, the dimension of justice. When the Holy Spirit animates preaching, one of its primary aims is to manifest justice in the earth. The anointing of the Spirit manifests power to heal, deliver, and change lives. It also seeks to manifest justice.

Luke is one of the major authors of the New Testament and a man who talked more about the work of the Holy Spirit than authors such as John, Peter and maybe Paul. For Luke, the work of the Holy Spirit has a larger aim than providing gifts to enhance Christian worship. The Spirit is about transforming the world with the gospel of Jesus Christ and a core part of that transformation means working toward a world where justice is present for the most vulnerable. One place in Luke's gospel where this emphasis is clear is in the inauguration of the ministry of Jesus. The anointing of the Spirit on his ministry has decided implications for special groups of people.

> *"The Spirit of the Lord is on me, because he has anointed me to proclaim good news to the poor. He has sent me to proclaim freedom for the prisoners and recovery of sight for the blind, to set the oppressed free, to proclaim the year of the Lord's favor"* (Luke 4:18-19, my translation).

When the Spirit came upon Jesus, it is important to take note of the concerns Jesus voiced because they are reflections of the work of the Spirit both on him and his followers. Jesus expresses concern for the poor, prisoners, the blind, and the oppressed. The Spirit cares deeply for these people. In addition to noting the fact that the Spirit shows concern for them, it is equally important to note the specific workings of the Spirit toward these people. The Spirit anointed Jesus to preach good news, to proclaim liberty, to give sight, and to set free. These are all workings that reflect a concern for justice.

One of the more popular parables in Luke 16 draws on the eschatological image of hell to address the problem of neglecting the poor.

> *There was a certain rich man who dressed in purple and fine clothes and feasted sumptuously every day. And a certain poor man named Lazarus was laid at his gate and covered with sores. And he longed to be fed with what fell from the rich man's table and the dogs came and licked his sores. But it came to be that the poor man died and was carried by the angels to Abraham's bosom. And the rich man died also and was buried. And in hell, he lifted up his eyes in severe pain and saw Abraham from a distance and Lazarus in his bosom. And he called out, Father Abraham, have mercy on me, and send Lazarus to dip the tip of his finger in water and cool my tongue, for I am in pain in this flame. But Abraham said, Son remember that you received good things in your life, and Lazarus in like manner received bad things; but now he is being comforted here and you suffer pain* (Lk 16:19-25).

In this passage, we are introduced to two persons who led very different lives. The rich man fared well in this life. In verses 19-20, we are told that he dressed in purple and fine linen, feasted sumptuously every day, and a poor man was laid at his gate. In contrast to the good life that the rich man lived, Lazarus, the other person in the story, did not fare well. In verses 20-21 we find that Lazarus is crippled, poor, covered with sores, hungry, and consoled only by the dogs that licked his sores.

Luke uses the contrast in their lives to emphasize the dramatic reversal they will experience in the afterlife. There are two persons in the story: one is very rich and the other is very poor. One person experiences joy in this life while the other lives in misery. He does this because reversal is an important theological issue. In the Lucan account of the teachings of Jesus, the last in this life will be first and the first in this life will be last or left out altogether (13:22-30). Abraham reminded the rich man of this very fact in verse 25 when he said, "Son remember that in this life you received your good things"- fine clothes, lavish feasts, and neglect of the poor- "and Lazarus in like manner bad things"- crippled, poor, sick, hungry.

Because of these very different lives, Abraham explains to the rich man that "now he (Lazarus) is comforted and you suffer pain." Luke draws the stark contrast of their fates in the afterlife, employing the apocalyptic image of hell, from the Greek word Hades which in ancient literature refers to the underworld, the nether world, or the place of departed spirits. Interestingly, both the rich man and Lazarus live in this other realm called Hades but lead different lives. In Hades,

Lazarus is comforted (in Abraham's bosom) while the rich man suffers pain.

One of the main points in the story is to point out the implications of neglecting the poor, which is a social justice concern. God cares about the poor and wants his people to share his concern and their means to alleviate their suffering. Scholars often focus on Luke's interest in the poor and critique of the rich as major literary themes. For example, in 6:20, 24, Jesus pronounces a blessing on the poor and promises them the kingdom of God and woe to the rich because they have already received comfort. The story of the rich fool in 12:15-21, the admonition that no person can serve two masters (God and mammon) in 16:13, and the story of the rich young ruler in 18:18-27 are examples of this theme. In Luke 16, God, in the person of Abraham, condemns the rich man for neglecting Lazarus. In fact, the gospel of Luke is an indictment against wealth that is not mindful of those who are less fortunate. Look at the multiple examples of Jesus helping those who were unable to help themselves in the gospel of Luke.

- 4:18 declaration that his mission was for the poor, the oppressed, the blind;
- 4:38 healing of Simon's mother-in-law;
- 5:12 cleansing of a leper;
- 5:17 healing of a paralytic;
- 6:6 healing of a man with a withered hand;
- 7:11 raising of a widow's son;

- 7:22 proof of the advent of the kingdom was good works to those in need;
- 7:36 forgiving the woman;
- 8:26 healing (exorcism) of Gaderene demoniac;
- 8:40 raising of Jairus' daughter;
- 9:10 feeding of five thousand;
- 10:25 good Samaritan's help to one in need;
- 15:11 forgiveness and restoration of the lost son;
- 23:34 Jesus' prayer of forgiveness on the cross.

Luke provides such an abundance of examples so that those who choose to follow Jesus have a guide as to what it means to be a disciple. In writings that are heavily concerned with the machinations of the Holy Spirit, I don't understand why readers miss the larger concerns for justice in the gospels and Acts. Luke writes in a way that lets readers know, when the Spirit is on you, the same concerns Jesus had for the poor, for prisoners, for the blind and oppressed will be your concerns.

One problem we have is the preachers who want to spiritualize social issues such as poverty in Luke and focus only on the need for repentance and forgiveness of sins, which are other important themes in Luke. How can you spiritualize poverty in Luke when he is so clear that one of the central concerns of Jesus was to care for the poor and downcast? It is important that true spirituality is not misconstrued. The only spiritual application that we should take from Luke's gospel is to take seriously the call to meet the basic needs of people, especially those unable (for whatever reason) to do so for themselves.

These concerns from the Holy Spirit should ground our preaching and ministries. So now I ask, "What is Spirit-filled social justice preaching?" First, it is preaching that speaks the good news of Jesus Christ and the message of the kingdom of God to people who live according to the fallen social structures and systems of the world.

This kind of preaching draws clears lines between values of these respective kingdoms and invites people into a vision of humanity where all people can flourish. This kind of preaching reminds the powerful that the structures of the world are a part of this present evil age that is passing away and is under the judgment of God. It is preaching that claims a new kingdom has dawned in the world and we give witness to its existence and invitation that is extended to all. More importantly, it is preaching that will challenge and expose the systems and power structures in the world that exploit and marginalize people. People suffer because of these systems and their suffering is against God's vision for their lives. So Spirit-filled justice preaching will challenge and expose the systems and power structures that exploit and marginalize people in the pulpit, in the streets, and in the halls and meetings rooms of power.

Second, it is preaching that draws on the gifts of the Spirit to give knowledge (insight), strength, and wisdom (discernment) to believers to more fully participate in this work. The Spirit anoints and equips people, enabling them to effectively do the works of God. This kind of preaching participates in a larger program inaugurated by God when He sent Jesus to earth two thousand years ago and will culminate in His return to earth. This work has a personal dimension, a congregational dimension, and a social dimension. The Spirit will use gifts for sermons, for church and social ministries, wisdom to share with community leaders and discernment to navigate the challenges of justice work whether it's personal ideas, bills being voted on in congress or the senate, programs or new companies funded by major corporations, etc. The Spirit will guide and at times give words to you to speak.

Third, it is preaching that transforms minds and hearts as it relates to how people see others, especially the vulnerable. An important part of ministry is cultivating empathy in God's people so they not only do the work but care about the people doing the work and people who need ministry. I cannot overstate how important this is and how it is work that the Spirit does in good preaching and teaching. Preachers are partners with the Spirit in this. For example, the Spirit will lead us to preach to cultivate compassion and care for the poor and for people who are different. Without genuine compassion for people, their ministry and care will be ineffective and in many instances non-existent. In Luke, Jesus meets a man named Zacchaeus. He was a tax collector and hated by many in Jericho. This didn't stop Jesus from having dinner with him. Because of this, Zacchaeus made some decisions that night that changed his life and the lives of others.

> *But Zacchaeus stood up and said to the Lord, Lord, Lord! Here and now I give half of my possessions to the poor, and if I have cheated anybody out of anything, I will pay back four times the amount. Jesus said to him, today salvation has come to this house, because this man, too, is a son of Abraham. For the Son of Man came to seek and to save what was lost* (Lk 19:8-10, NIV).

The salvation he experienced that night was not merely from all his sins but in particular the sins that caused him to take advantage of and defraud others. He was saved from that and sought restitution. This is one of the most powerful accounts of conversion in the Bible because it shows a person can be saved from the love of money and privilege from an exploitative system.

Luke gives this story and the parables of the lost sheep and son to emphasize the importance of one's disposition toward others. How we look at people in the world affects our ability to ministry to them. And this is a primary concern of the Spirit and preaching that speaks to justice issues. I believe there are different kinds of social justice preaching. I would not characterize all of it as Christian in the truest sense. There are preachers who preach justice but do so with hate in their hearts for the people who marginalize and exploit others. While I commend them for speaking up for those who do not have voice in society, preaching with hate in one's heart for others in the name of justice does not bring salvation to the world, it brings more division. As hard as it is to imagine, Jesus cares about the vulnerable and also about those who exploit them. He wants to save them both and invite them into communion with Him and one another.

Martin Luther King, Jr. was a preacher like this. He believed in racial and economic justice. He was a strident critic of America's injustice in these areas but he did not preach with hate in his heart for whites. He preached the truth and did it with love for the very people who worked to undermine his efforts and oppress him.

Why would I say this? One of the great temptations in fighting systemic evil is attempting to do so in one's own power. Doing this is a grave mistake because what can happen is giving in to another form of evil while trying to fight evil in the first place. Luke insists that disciples need to be empowered by the Spirit. Jesus was adamant about this in both Luke and Acts. It is a belief shared by many Pentecostals and Charismatics.

Bishop Ithiel Clemmons in his book on Bishop C. H. Mason and the origins of the Church of God in Christ expressed his concern for his Baptist and Methodist sisters and brothers who were trying to fight the demons of racism without the power of the Holy Spirit.[11] Mason did not believe that such evil could be engaged and defeated by human intelligence, human will, and human effort alone. This work requires human intelligence, will, and effort fused with the power of God. Otherwise, one may

---

[11] Ithiel Clemmons, *Bishop C. H Mason and the Roots of the Church of God in Christ* (Pneuma Life Publishing, 1996), 19.

be consumed by the very evil they seek to overcome. These three things describe the essence of Spirit-filled social justice preaching.

The third principle of Spirit filled preaching is that preaching inevitably has a mysterious dimension to it. What I mean by mysterious is that there are things that happen in the preaching experience that is sometimes hard to explain. The Holy Spirit uses the preacher and his words in ways he or she cannot fully understand. For example, congregants can hear things in the sermon that you intended to say. They also hear through their own understanding of God, the Bible, and life.

There are times when the Spirit gives insight and inspiration in the preaching moment that you did not expect or prepare for as you crafted the sermon. Spiritual things happen in the preaching moment. Hearing sermons encompass the spiritual, cognitive, emotive, and existential. In other words, there is a difference between what you say in the sermon from how it may be heard. I have had people come up to me after a sermon and explain how they heard something I had said in an altogether different light. I thought to myself, "is that what I said?" What I have found is that the Spirit enables people to hear things germane to their life situations. There are things that I said that did not apply to their life situation in the way that I had intended but the Spirit gives them ears to hear its applicability in creative ways.

There is a mystery to preaching. Only the Spirit of God knows what people have been through and what is on their mind. So the Spirit speaks a word to the messenger of God from the word of God. It is impossible to speak a word that is immediately applicable to all the different people in church. But the Spirit can take certain ideas or points in the sermon and allow people to personally apply it in diverse ways.

> *And they were all filled with the Holy Spirit and began to speak in tongues as the Spirit gave them utterance. Now there were dwelling in Jerusalem Jews, devout men from every nation under heaven. And at this sound the multitude came together, and they were bewildered, because each one was hearing them speak in his own language* (Acts 2:4-6).

These verses in Acts 2 describe the mysterious miraculous ability to hear different things. People on the day of Pentecost were speaking in different languages or tongues. But the wonder was in the hearing, not the speaking. I believe the same holds true in preaching. The mystery is in what is heard and not just what is said. This acknowledges the active role of the Spirit in the sermonic experience.

The fourth principle of Spirit filled preaching is that the word of God comes to the preacher. When a man or woman of God is in tune with the Spirit of God and the people of God, God sends you or gives you a word to preach. In the Old Testament when God gave a message to the prophets, the text says, "and the word of the Lord came to the prophet." God sends and gives words for his people. But too often preachers do not have a word from God. They have something good to say. They may even have something inspiring to say. But unless they have a word from God it will fail to make a substantive difference in the lives of God's people.

There are three essential principles to this belief: (1) God still speaks; (2) women and men of God must discern the voice of God; and (3) both the preacher and people must have ears to hear the word that comes from God. When God gave a word the prophets did not stand around and wonder whether or not God can still speak. God still speaks today. So many debate whether or not God still speaks because we have the Bible. That seems ridiculous to me. Why would God become silent? It was his voice and inspiration that gave us Scripture. I am not saying that God's voice and prophetic messages are normative like Scripture. Scripture is the canon and rule of faith for believers. But the fact that we have Scripture does not in any sense silence God. God is alive and well in the earth and still speaks to those who have ears to hear him. However, it is essential that one can discern what God is saying.

There is never a shortage of voices claiming to represent God. What's important is discernment. Believers need an ability to distinguish authentic voices and messages from false voices and messages. In the book of Corinthians Paul instructed that when inspired "prophetic" like messages are given, two or three should judge. I believe that in church there should be those members or leaders who judge or discern whether the preached word is a "word from the Lord." They should do so to make sure that a clear distinction between a good word and God word. Good words sound good and make you feel good but a God word can correct, challenge, and change your life. I am going to offer a few criteria to discern a good word from a God word.

1. *Does it glorify God? Is the impetus of the sermon centered on God's presence and will in the world?*
2. *Is it Christ centered in some manner? Does the message connect with the life, teachings, death, and resurrection of Jesus Christ in a real way?*
3. *Does the message resonate with God's dealings with Israel and other peoples and nations recorded in Scripture?*
4. *Does the message challenge those whose lives do not measure up to Christian standards to make some changes?*
5. *Does the message offer comfort and encouragement to those who have suffered or are persecuted?*
6. *Does the message call for an authentic response to God in repentance, prayer, worship, or service to others which leads to both personal and communal transformation?*

Conclusion

Spiritual preaching has breadth in that it addresses existential, eternal, and social issues. Spiritual preaching has depth in that it exposes the reasons people are in bondage to vices that rob them of true joy and hurt others around them, it interrogates reasons why people are not concerned with eternal matters, why people are invested in systems that exploit others and how to live into the inclusive vision of God's kingdom. This kind of preaching, preaching that deals with the heart of the gospel can strengthen and revitalize the church. I hope that such matters will occupy the imagination of this and the next generation of preachers and not so much the artistic dimensions- how to get the people excited, how to make people shout, and how to impress other preachers. The preoccupation on the art of preaching is stifling our churches and producing preachers who preach the good news of Jesus for all the wrong reasons.

Chapter Three

The Two Challenges for Contemporary Preachers

There are two great challenges before the preacher. Preachers must wrestle with and speak the truth of God in a world that refuses to acknowledge God's truth and they must also do so in congregations that refuse to live into God's vision of peace and justice for the world.

Preachers must also discern the best way to express the truth of God in the moments of life. There are times for preaching and times for teaching. This is where preachers are experiencing problems. Speaking the truth consistently and learning to balance preaching and teaching both present challenges to the preacher's spirituality and discernment.

Tell the Truth Preacher

Maybe one of the most difficult aspects of preaching is telling the truth at all times. Now this sounds like it may not be difficult but there is more to this than one may initially think. One may respond, "Of course the preacher must speak the truth. That is a no brainer." I agree but telling the truth extends far beyond the preaching moment on Sunday. Certainly, it encompasses the whole of the preacher's life and challenges whether he or she brings boldness and integrity to the preaching task. Speaking truth in preaching deals with the very core of the preacher's personhood. It necessitates that the preacher has an inner spiritual soundness that helps him or her remain faithful throughout the duration of their ministry.

Paul tried to convey this to a young pastor he mentored named Timothy. He wanted Timothy to stay faithful to preaching the word at all times and not being swayed by the whims of fickle people who don't always want to hear the truth.

> *I charge thee therefore before God and the Lord Jesus Christ, who shall judge the quick and the dead at his appearing and his kingdom; preach the word, be instant in season, out of season; reprove, rebuke, exhort with all longsuffering and doctrine. For the time will come when they will not endure sound doctrine, but after their own lusts shall they heap to themselves, having itching ears; and they shall turn their ears away from the truth and be turned to fables. But watch thou in all things, endure afflictions, do the work of an evangelist, make full proof of thy ministry*
> (2 Tim 4:1-5).

Notice how Paul exhorts this pastor to be watchful, to endure afflictions, and to do the work of an evangelist. This exhortation reveals that a part of the preaching ministry requires watchfulness about how one goes about this work, lest they get caught up in the fads and changing trends of the world. This watchfulness and careful approach to the calling of preaching will bring suffering. He described some of the suffering in verses 3-4. People are not always receptive to the truth and will seek teachers who will tell them what they want to hear. This is not an easy thing to deal with as a preacher and is why the temptation to compromise, dilute, or change the message is so strong. Rejection and isolation are common experiences among clergy who are faithful truth tellers and these experiences complicate our ability to continue telling the truth because it is difficult to separate the rejection of the message from the rejection of the messenger. My friend, speaking truth is a serious and complex issue in preaching. Let's unpack some of these things.

I will begin with holy boldness, another term for courage. Preachers must be courageous. Speaking truth in preaching means one has to instruct and challenge the people when there is sin in the camp or challenge the church to deal with issues they'd rather ignore. This is especially difficult to do with those who are supportive of you. You have to tell them the truth also because some may befriend the preacher in an attempt to silence him or her in regards to their sin or sins or an issue they may not agree with.

Speaking the truth means challenging the church to line up with God's vision of righteousness and justice for everyone. Speaking truth issues a challenge to everyone in the church who has their own agenda to make sure that it does not usurp God's agenda. A preacher must courageously bring correction and instruction even when people do not see error or worse yet when they refuse to acknowledge that they need change. Without courage the preacher sees sin and error and yet ignores it in the preaching moment.

Without courage the preacher will be more concerned with job security and being liked by the congregants instead of fidelity to truth, and therefore will avoid truth speaking when it threatens this. Courage and boldness ought to be the resource most frequently drawn on by the preacher. One speaks the truth in love and if it costs him or her their job or a pseudo supporter then so be it. But the truth of God cannot and should not be domesticated by any person, group, or constituency in the church. Faithful preaching requires the preacher not to allow the word of God to be controlled or manipulated by anyone or any agenda.

Speaking the truth in love requires boldness rooted in a radical commitment to God and truth. However, the ability to remain faithful to this throughout one's ministry requires integrity. If a preacher has integrity they will speak the truth at all times, knowing how difficult such a task is and knowing that there may be consequences for doing so from those who hate or reject the truth. If a preacher lacks integrity, he or she can easily be deceived. It is important to not only tell the church the truth; the preacher must tell himself or herself the truth.

One of the things that make me laugh is to hear preachers blasting everyone else's sin and problems while unwittingly ignoring their own sin and problems. Faithful preaching ought to challenge and humble the preacher because the truth should cut both ways. It should bring correction to the people and the messenger. But here is where deception can sneak in. The ability to preach and hear from God in no way exempts the preacher from the requirement of living out the gospel nor does it mean that the preacher does not himself or herself need to apply the word to their lives. Just because one preaches or is the spokesperson of God, the congregants can unwittingly think that the preacher has it all together, especially when their insight is so profound. This omission can tempt the preacher to deceive himself. Preaching with integrity requires balance. One must faithfully exegete the church and oneself so as to speak a true word to all. A preacher can go wrong when they fall into thinking that the word is for the people and not the preacher. If one does not practice what one preaches then there is little to no integrity in preaching.

A part of the difficult task of preaching is self-correction, self-challenge, and reverent self-examination. It is hard to tell yourself the truth at all times, especially in the preaching moment. Doing so requires that the tight rope between pride and humility be carefully walked. But one has to have integrity to continually subject oneself to this process because the easy thing to do is to focus on performance preaching. Again self-deception must be addressed. Profound insight and understanding does not mean the preacher's life is parallel to his or her understanding. Great preaching ability can be present with significant integrity and morality gaps in the preacher's life.

That is why it is essential for the preacher to practice the spiritual disciplines. There is so much more to preaching than what goes on at the eleven o'clock hour. That is only the capstone. If the preacher has integrity and exemplifies true spirituality then their sermons and their life will be bathed in prayer, meditation, and accountability. In order to stand tall in the pulpit one has to have moral authority. Moral authority comes from a life of prayer, holiness (dedication to God), and consistency. I did not say perfection but consistency because preachers are not perfect. This kind of lifestyle implies that there is a consistency to the preacher's life that gives the moral base and authority to preach the truth. This is important. Even when the preaching moment requires you to deal with areas where you struggle, if your spiritual life is honest, consistent, and growing then you have the moral authority to preach with power and conviction. If not then the preaching moment is tainted with insincerity and worse yet, hypocrisy. Preachers have to commit to the Christian life in order to effectively preach to the people about the benefits of faithfulness and liabilities of unfaithfulness.

Again that is why I emphasize the importance of the spirituality of preaching. Preaching is based on spiritual power and not just human wisdom or ability. One reason preaching has become ineffective is its reliance on human ability and not spiritual power. But how can one operate with spiritual power when their spiritual life is deficient and in some cases nonexistent. A nonexistent or deficient spiritual life leaves spiritual and moral gaps unattended to. Yet the weekly preaching continues. And when this cycle sets in, preaching becomes perfunctory and devoid of power because it has no moral or spiritual base. The preacher then begins to preach at people and to preach informative sermons that are noticeably devoid of transformative power. Paul warned that in the last days, people would have a form of godliness but deny its power and efficacy in their lives. Well those days are here. In conclusion, the goal of good preaching is the synthesis of revelatory God inspired insight into preaching and the living of the gospel. God gave us his word so that all God's children will walk in the light and grow in the areas where the light is not shining.

The gospel is about God's truth challenging the lies that the fallen world is built upon. This means that Christian preaching is always and unavoidably confrontational. If you want to be liked and popular then you may not want to be a Christian preacher because preaching means telling the truth and exposing lies. What causes confrontation is when what the gospel calls a lie is believed as absolute truth by a person or persons, communities, and sometimes entire nations. Lies such as God created humans and divided them into different races of people is a lie that countries make an absolute truth and construct societies and policies to reinforce. Christian preaching must challenge these lies.

The preacher's job is to hold up for the world the truth of God. One way to do this is to follow the Great Commission as recorded in Matthew 28. In Matthew Jesus commissions his disciples to go and teach all nations "baptizing them in the name of the Father, and of the Son, and of the Holy Spirit." In addition, he instructs his disciples to teach them "all things, whatsoever I have commanded." In essence, Jesus says, go and share with the world what I have taught you. In this sense, the truth of God can be represented in the teachings of Jesus.

Balancing Teaching and Preaching

One of the important things to balance as a pastor is the wisdom and ability to know when to preach and when to teach. There is a time to preach and a time to teach. There is a time for inspiring proclamation and a time for careful explanation. There are different words in the New Testament for preaching (kerusso) and teaching (didasko). I will admit at the outset of this essay that my interpretation of Ephesians 4:11 informs my belief that pastors must preach and teach. Effective pastors have gifts to proclaim and explain. These men and women are gifts like apostles, prophets, and evangelists. Pastor-teachers or pastors who are preacher-teachers are gifts to the church to edify it.

One of the more unfortunate developments in contemporary preaching is the tendency to give the people what they want instead of what God wants. This is nothing new. Paul warned Timothy about this two thousand years ago in 2 Timothy 4. While not new, the shape of this trend is having an influence on preachers and churches. The seeker sensitive movement and American consumerist philosophy that the "customer" is always right has resulted in a culture of churches that feel pressured to cater to people and give them what they want to become their church of choice.

To some extent, people come to church expecting it to give them what they want and if they don't like it, they'll find another church. This is what Paul warned Timothy about, people with "itching ears" who want preachers to tell them what they want to hear. The religious market has even affected the way they want the message delivered. There has been a bit of a dichotomy and rivalry in the church about preaching and teaching gifts. And too many preachers give in to unrealistic and unscriptural beliefs about preaching and teaching.

Among predominately African American churches, there is a real tension and history of disrespect between the preaching and teaching gifts. I have seen this played out in my twenty-three years of ministry in African American Pentecostal, nondenominational, Baptist, and Presbyterian churches. Some churches want preachers. Some want teachers. It is kind of like a box that a preacher must fit into depending on the church. For those of us with the dual gift to preach and teach, it is challenging to fit into those boxes. Let me explain this.

There is a long tradition in the Black Church of effective and charismatic preachers who are gifted orators. Martin Luther King, Jr. is an example of this tradition. His skillful use of words and engaging cadences captivated a nation during a difficult time in history. Vashti McKenzie, Jeremiah Wright, T. D. Jakes, Jasmine Sculark, Freddie Haynes, and Gina Stewart are all exceptional contemporary black preachers and a part of the long history of great preachers. This tradition's influence is so strong that teaching pastors and teaching scholars are not viewed with the same reverence.

Younger preachers who want to be more "successful" sometimes pattern their preaching after these homiletical luminaries. "I want to be the next great preacher that gets all the speaking engagements and preaches to packed houses nationally." That statement is something you're likely to hear in hallways at major conferences or over dinner tables as preachers shoot the breeze and fellowship. Preaching is the lifeblood of so many black churches and the more dynamic you are the more notoriety you can acquire. Preachers who are on the outside see this and some want it for themselves. So they reason, the best way to get there is to preach like they do.

    This is problematic for many reasons. First, the preacher will become focused on homiletical style or brand because they are trying to position themselves to succeed in the preaching market. Matters of preaching style are important but should not be the focus of the preacher, particularly younger preachers. Their focus should be on developing and building basic skills in ministry and strengthening their walk with God. Second, preachers may use current preaching opportunities as practice instead of opportunities to feed the flock. Instead of viewing preaching as sacred opportunities to feed the people of God and inspire them to good works, some use it as practice sessions.

    Let me explain this. There is a praxis element to preaching. In most cases, the more one preaches the better one becomes. So in a sense the practice of preaching weekly improves the skills of the preacher. That is a basic fact of preaching. But that is not what I am critiquing because their focus is on the sacred task of preaching to God's people and not on how to use preaching opportunities as stepping stones to greater venues. Third, preachers will not develop their own identity as a preacher. The preoccupation with effective and very popular preachers can be tempting toward mimicry instead of undertaking the long process of developing one's own sense of identity and style. As long as impressionable preachers are mimicking other preachers when they preach they are not developing as preachers.

Arguably the biggest problem with this is for those who teach. Seminary, divinity school, university, or college teachers of religion and philosophy as well as teaching pastors are not given the same respect. They are relegated to lesser significance and value in many black churches. They are not given the same opportunities to speak to congregations as preachers. Many times they are not invited to participate at all. They are not invited as keynote speakers in the same way as preachers. And many times they are paid significantly smaller amounts than preachers. I have seen this in my own ministry.

When I was a pastor, there were multiple opportunities to speak to churches and exercise leadership. Now that I am both a scholar and preacher, there are less opportunities in the church for my gifts. I rarely receive invitations to teach in the church. My invitations are to preach, because I was a preacher years before I became a scholar. And sadly, the few times I am invited to lecture, churches do not want to pay me for the extensive time it takes to write a lecture or lesson and when they do pay it is meager to say the least. It is significantly less than I get for preaching engagements. I have many colleagues who are both scholars and preachers. They experience the same thing.

This does two things to younger preachers. First, aspiring preachers see this and it affects their vocational aspirations. Second, the climate of disrespect puts pressure on some preachers to try to fit into the preaching mold and neglect teaching altogether. There are, however, exceptions to this in Word of Faith and nondenominational churches. There is more value placed on teaching and these churches may represent a growing edge for predominately African American churches. Even though some of these teachers pastor large churches in major cities, they are not considered top black preachers. When major conferences are held throughout the country or even revivals in local communities, the keynote speaker is still a preacher and not a teacher.

Admittedly, some of this is a false dichotomy and should not be taken to extremes. It is important to discuss the different ways preaching and teaching are received in the contemporary Black Church but there are a few caveats needed so as not to overstate my case. First, it is important to note that many of the top preachers blend teaching and preaching elements. Just because someone is a preacher does not mean they don't teach in their sermons. Many do but would still self-identify as a preacher. Second, while teachers may struggle for opportunities to teach in black churches that does not mean these churches are bereft of teaching. Even though the New Testament differentiates between preaching and teaching, sermons can have elements of both depending on the gifts and style of the preacher.

Many times, pastors who may self-identify as a preacher teach Sunday school classes, Bible study lessons, and sermonic segments that teach. Third, some people have only preaching or teaching gifts. There are preachers who are not gifted teachers and there are teachers who are not gifted preachers. They should not feel pressure to do what they are not gifted for or called to do. They should faithfully exercise their gifts.

> *"Now there are diversities of gifts, but the same Spirit and there are differences of administrations, but the same Lord. And there are diversities of operations, but it is the same God which worketh in all…are all apostles? Are all prophets (preachers)? Are all teachers? (1 Cor 12:4-6, 29).*

Paul is clear that in the church or the body of Christ, there are different gifts and operations called on to edify the church. There is nothing wrong with only having a preaching gift. There is nothing wrong with only having a teaching gift. What's important is to recognize both gifts and equally value them instead of pitting them against one another in the church. This was the same flawed logic that Paul corrected in his letter to the Corinthians.

Rejecting the False Preacher-Teacher Dichotomy

Preaching, if it is faithful, must arise out of what God has impressed on the preacher's heart to share and burned on the preacher's mind to proclaim. God gives messages or words to preachers and teachers. In the Bible, sermons are sometimes called a "word" or "words" from the Lord. God would give "words" to the prophets and God incarnate would teach in parables so people could understand the mysteries of the kingdom. The messages that God gives require both the preaching and teaching gift to be employed to ensure maximum effectiveness. But the temptation for a pastor who relies more on one gift than the other is to completely ignore the need to utilize the other gift when necessary, even if it means inviting someone with that gift to the church. For example, a great preacher can be so good at preaching that his or her congregation becomes overly dependent on preaching to the extent that they cannot receive a word from God unless it is preached. I have seen churches fall in love and become addicted to preaching so much so that the teaching gift is relegated to second-class status. In these kind of churches anyone who teaches only does so because they obviously cannot preach. Nothing could be further from the truth.

    I have also seen the same thing in churches where the pastor almost always teaches. Teaching pastors break the word down and explain things in ways that is different than preaching. Unfortunately, what happens is that the people grow to love teaching and view preaching in a less than flattering manner. Preaching is viewed in these teaching churches as emotional talk not rooted in scripture and that people get excited about preaching but do not understand why. Again, nothing could be further from the truth. I look forward to the day when the church values and receives both the preaching and teaching gifts. Until both gifts are recognized as equal gifts of communication for pastors, women and men of God will continue to struggle to find balance. Pastors have to challenge such erroneous thinking in their churches and lead churches to appreciate both gifts.

Struggling for Balance

Let's go deeper. Many, not all, pastors have the dual gift to preach and teach. Many have both but may do one better than the other. If God calls them to a church that places a premium on one gift the temptation will be to give in to the pressure to perform or please the people, especially if what they like is your strong gift. Serving a church is likened in Scripture to being a shepherd.

One of the requirements of the shepherd is feeding the sheep. A good shepherd makes sure the sheep eats what is best for them and not what they would like to eat. Too many pastors lack the spiritual maturity and spiritual will to care for the people of God. God knows what is best for the people and based on that knowledge, he reveals to the man and woman of God what "thus saith the Lord." But if the pastor continually subjects himself or herself to the pressures to perform and give the people what they want, the gifts and power of God are significantly diluted. If God gives a word that requires instruction, the pastor must teach with simplicity so the people will have understanding even if they are largely accustomed to preaching.

Conclusion

There is so more to effective pastoral leadership than the preaching experience and there is more to preaching than finding a text and explaining it to the people. Preaching is rooted in the call of God and conviction that God's people live by God's word. And so pastors study the word and commune with God so as to be able to share biblical revelation and its relevance for today. Effective communication in the church can no longer be bound by the petty entertainment impetus present in so many churches. God is calling pastors who are willing to express their love for God by feeding and caring for the flock of God. In order to carry out this mandate pastors need to exercise the dual gifts of preaching and teaching. Paul's instructions to young pastors in 1-2 Timothy and Titus placed a premium on both the ability to teach and to preach (see 1 Tim 3:2; Tit 1:9; 2 Tim 4:1-5).

    Men and women of God need five things in order to balance the teaching and preaching responsibilities of their call. Pastors need a functional spirituality in order to faithfully execute the call to share God's truth. Pastors need wisdom and discernment to know when to preach and when to teach. Pastors need strength not to succumb to the pressure of giving the people what they want. Pastors need spiritual sensitivity to hear God's voice and lead the people based on what you hear. Pastors need love to feed the flock of God a balanced diet of instruction and inspiration that empowers and encourages. The pastor must know the people and their needs through spiritual discernment, prayer, and fellowship in order to effectively speak into their lives.

Chapter Four

The Preacher as Worshipper

Years ago in many black churches it was a common ritual for the pastor to sing a song or hymn before preaching the sermon. This was known as the pre-sermonic hymn and it was not sung by the choir but by the preacher. It is not too long but rather a short song is delivered in worship to God and a way to bring focus to God; who is preparing to speak to the people of God through the preacher. I grew up in a small Black Church in Kimball, West Virginia and it was common for my pastor overseer Arnie H. Joyce to sing a verse or two of a song before preaching. I remember my uncle Elder Benjamin Brogdon who pastored Mt. Harmon Branch Holiness Church of God, Inc. He used to sing, "Jesus is the best thing that happened to me." The praises to God would fill that small church in Thorpe, West Virginia. Pastors who were not gifted singers or who did not want to strain their voice, after maybe a week of preaching a revival, would invite soloist to sing a verse for them. It was important that the preaching moment began with a song, a sacred moment of worship and consecration.

For years growing up in church I did not understand why the preacher had to sing another song. Why couldn't he or she just start the sermon? At times the worship and joy erupted into ecstatic worship and shouting, only prolonging the service. I am ashamed to admit that I used to think, "here we go again." Back then, I didn't understand why it was important for the preacher to worship God before the sermon, but I do now. I appreciate the many preachers who lifted up God's amazing grace and his son Jesus Christ who is a friend to the friendless and mother to the motherless before the preaching moment.

The pre-sermonic hymn served an important function in Black Church worship during this time. In a tradition with dynamic and gifted preaching, it was essential for the preacher to lift up God on one hand and humble him or herself for the task of preaching to the people of God on the other. It was a way for the preacher to acknowledge that the glory and praise belongs to God, no matter how profound and moving a sermon would follow. And it was worth the extra time in worship because it was good for people not to get confused and caught up in the preaching moment thinking the glory and gifts on display were because of human excellence. I miss those pre-sermonic hymns today from men and women of God who desired to humble themselves before God and the people of God in the preaching moment. This ritual has fallen on hard times in the Black Church. Today there is little worship of God by popular preachers and not much of an acknowledgement of his glory and presence in the preaching moment. There is no time for that. The preacher has to start the performance.

A part of the crisis of entertainment preaching is a failure of preachers to worship the God they preach about. This is both a product of major changes in worship in black churches and also changes in how black preachers see themselves. Many black churches have shifted from a theo-centric model of worship to one that is preacher-centric. Much of what goes on in Black Church worship leads up to the preacher and preaching moment. Preachers are the stars, the main attraction. This is what has become central. God has become ancillary and relegated to a secondary status. God is talked about but not worshipped as a living presence amidst his people. It is arguable if much of what passes as worship in black churches is theo-centric. The central role pastors and preachers have in worship reflects a preacher-centric culture and theology.

One reason preaching has become a show is that preachers do not worship God, especially in public worship. The more I travel to major conferences and churches the more apparent it is that preachers have lost their love of worship. It is rare to see a preacher worship God in a worship service. Many sit and look important throughout worship and do not praise God until they have a microphone in their hand. Some can even be seen reading text messages on their phones and being served by armor bearers or nurse aids. There are even those who stay in their study until it is almost time to preach. When they enter, the worship service stops and everyone stands to reverence them as they walk to the pulpit. There is something deeply wrong with the culture of churches that preachers have become so high and lifted up in the space set aside for the worship of God. It was attitudes and practices like these among leaders that infuriated Jesus. He was very critical of the Pharisees and Scribes for the way they took advantage of their positions as religious leaders to draw attention to themselves.

> *Then spake Jesus to the multitude, and to his disciples, Saying the scribes and the Pharisees sit in Moses' seat: All therefore whatsoever they bid you observe, that observe and do; but do not ye after their works: for they say, and do not. For they bind heavy burdens and grievous to be borne, and lay them on men's shoulders; but they themselves will not move them with one of their fingers. But all their works they do for to be seen of men: they make broad their phylacteries, and enlarge the borders of their garments, and love the uppermost rooms at feasts, and the chief seats in the synagogues, and greetings in the markets, and to be called of men, Rabbi, Rabbi. But be not ye called Rabbi: for one is your Master, even Christ; and all ye are brethren. And call no man your father upon the earth: for one is your Father, which is in heaven. Neither be ye called masters: for one is your Master, even Christ. But he that is greatest among you shall be your servant. And whosoever shall exalt himself shall be abased; and he that shall humble himself shall be exalted* (Matt 23:1-12).

Jesus said they "love the uppermost rooms at feasts and the chief seats in the synagogues." They loved the honor and attention that came with being a religious leader. It looks like they loved it too much and forgot their place in the world. I can't help but wonder what Jesus would say if he attended Black Church conferences to hear the big name preachers who sit in the seat of honor or the preacher who leads the popular church in town. I wonder what he'd say about what he would see and if he would notice that preachers don't worship the God they preach about until it is time for them to preach.

The preacher as worshipper is a lost practice in today's Black Church. This has to change. I actually feel out of place as I attend and preach in churches because I am a worshiper. It doesn't matter what the denomination is, I come to church to worship God, not to be important. I stand in reverence of God's presence. I sing and raise my hands in worship to God. I verbalize praise to God. Then I get up to preach. It is important that I acknowledge God and worship God with the people I preach to because I want people to know it's all about God, not me. Some people in these churches look at me like there is something wrong with me. "Why is he standing up?" "Why is he singing?" "Why is he raising his hands?" There is something strange about preachers worshipping God in the culture of today's church. I long for the day when this is not the exception but rather the norm. I long for the day when people are surprised that the preacher is not worshipping God.

If we are to change this trend, preachers have to see themselves as worshipers in the truest sense of the word. I say this because worship of God frames the proper context for preaching, not the gifted and dynamic preacher seeking to impress the people with rhetorical and intellectual skill. The preaching moment is about God and God's people. It is not a show. It is not a stage for the preacher. It is actually a stage for God to show up and speak through yielded and imperfect vessels called preachers. Preachers must recover the spirituality that undergirds effective preaching.

Spiritual preaching comes from preachers with a healthy spirituality that manifests itself in men and women who worship God. In fact, worship is the preacher's first ministry because the end of everything that we do is to bring God glory. When preachers worship God it helps them to know their place in the world. Preachers need to know they are a small part of God's much larger order and plan for the ages. David realized this in Psalms 8:1-9

> *O LORD, our Lord, how excellent is thy name in all the earth! Who hast set thy glory above the heavens. ² Out of the mouth of babes and sucklings hast thou ordained strength because of thine enemies, that thou mightest still the enemy and the avenger. ³ When I consider thy heavens, the work of thy fingers, the moon and the stars, which thou hast ordained; ⁴ What is man, that thou art mindful of him? And the son of man, that thou visitest him? ⁵ For thou hast made him a little lower than the angels, and hast crowned him with glory and honour. ⁶ Thou madest him to have dominion over the works of thy hands; thou hast put all things under his feet: ⁷ All sheep and oxen, yea, and the beasts of the field; ⁸ The fowl of the air, and the fish of the sea, and whatsoever passeth through the paths of*

> the seas. ⁹ O L<small>ORD</small> our Lord, how excellent is thy name in all the earth!

He looked upon creation and marveled at Gods handiwork. He also marveled that God is mindful of humanity. David is not a preacher but was a leader before God's people and recognized his place. He was humbled by it. Paul did the same thing in Ephesians 3:1-8

> *For this cause I Paul, the prisoner of Jesus Christ for you Gentiles, If ye have heard of the dispensation of the grace of God which is given me to you-ward: How that by revelation he made known unto me the mystery; (as I wrote afore in few words, Whereby, when ye read, ye may understand my knowledge in the mystery of Christ) Which in other ages was not made known unto the sons of men, as it is now revealed unto his holy apostles and prophets by the Spirit; That the Gentiles should be fellow heirs and of the same body, and partakers of his promise in Christ by the gospel: Whereof I was made a minister, according to the gift of the grace of God given unto me by the effectual working of his power. Unto me, who am less than the least of all saints, is this grace given, that I should preach among the Gentiles the unsearchable riches of Christ*

Paul was in awe that God would reveal the mystery of Christ to him and make him a minister.

Paul considered himself less than the least of all saints. He didn't think of himself as a great apostle worthy to preach the unsearchable riches of Christ. He knew his place and was grateful to just be a minister. These kinds of attitudes are missing in the preaching ministry today. Imagine how one would approach the sermon moment if they had an attitude like David in Psalm 8 or Paul in Ephesians 3?

Spiritual preaching is connected to the preacher's view of him or herself. Worship helps you see yourself as you ought. When you know your place in creation it gives you a right view of yourself as a preacher. So how do you get a right view of yourself? Begin by revisiting the call of God. Every preacher should remember the attitude they had when God first called them. I worked in a seminary for eight years and talked to countless people about their call to ministry. Many were in discernment about their calling and not sure if God would call them to ministry. In those eight years, I cannot recall a single person who felt entitled about their call or that they were deserving of a call to ministry.

I never met a person who felt they were so important that God and the church needed them to be a minister. Most are surprised at God's call. They are deeply humbled and grateful to God for their call and for the encouragement and support they receive from their churches. But over the course of time in the ministry and maybe because of some of the benefits of being a minister, that attitude can change if one is not careful and disciplined. If this attitude was good enough when you first began ministry, why exchange it for the attitude of entitlement and pride that inundates the ministry today? Some preachers need to remember their call story.

In the Bible, God's call is a profound experience. It often overwhelmed prophets like Isaiah and Jeremiah and apostles like Peter and Paul. For example, Isaiah had a vision as a part of his call. In it he saw God sitting upon the throne, high and lifted up, and his train filled the Temple. He saw cherubim worshipping God and was so overwhelmed by God's holiness that he confessed, "Woe is me, for I am undone because I am a man of unclean lips and I dwell in the midst of a people with unclean lips: for mine eyes have seen the king, the Lord of hosts" (Is 6:5). Because of this confession, an angel put a coal upon his mouth and his iniquity was removed. He was able to go and speak for God. Peter heard Jesus preached on his boat to the crowds and after Jesus finished he told Peter to "cast his nets down." Peter responded by telling him he had toiled all night and caught nothing but would do as Jesus commanded. Soon after he caught so many fish that his net broke. Seeing this and remembering the words he heard Jesus speak, he confessed, "Depart from me for I am a sinful man, O Lord" (Lk 5:8).

These call stories paint a compelling picture and teach an invaluable and twofold lesson about the call to ministry. First, God is holy. God is above creation and crowned in glory. And to get a glimpse of his glory in any way is an overwhelming experience. Encountering a holy God is a terrifying and life-changing experience. Second, God calls unworthy and sinful people to do his will. Isaiah,

Jeremiah, Peter and Paul all had a sense of their unworthiness to preach or lead

God's people. They did so because of the way God called them. God's call often comes to us in ways that remind us of who God is and who we are in comparison. God is holy, all-wise, and all-powerful. We are unholy, foolish, and often powerless. Yet God calls us. I often think to myself before I get up to preach how unworthy I am to do what I am doing. I whisper a prayer of gratitude to God saying, "Thank you for letting me preach. I know I am not worthy." This is my way of staying grounded. This attitude of gratitude rooted in a profound recognition of one's place in creation, is one way to cultivate and strengthen the spiritual base upon which one engages in the task of ministry and out of which one ministers to their church and the larger community. This attitude also causes a fundamental shift in how the preacher engages God in worship and how the preacher models humility and gratitude, even in the worship space. What I am trying to say is that when a preacher has a right view of him or herself it will result in worship.

This is why I believe worship is the preacher's first ministry. The call to ministry comes from God and we hear and experience that call in a truly spiritual sense. God speaks and reveals and nurtures us through our call process and in spite of our disbelief, reluctance, hesitance, or fear we eventually accept it and move in faith and obedience to answer it. We pray and give thanks to God for the call and we bow in humble worship to the One who knew us before the foundation of the world and called us to be preachers. Before we ever preach or lead a church, we were in deep relationship of some kind with God. Before business cards were printed we were worshippers. Before we received important titles like "Bishop" or "Reverend" we bowed before God. We did this because worship was our first ministry and out of the wellspring of our worship of God we entered and engaged the task of ministry. But the temptation to forsake or to completely ignore this important ministry is strong and many succumb.

    One of my old pastors, then Elder, now Bishop Malverse Simpson of Roanoke, Virginia, used to tell his associate ministers that we should not get so caught up in the work of ministry that we forget the Lord of the work. He reminded us that in throws of ministry it easy to forget who called us and why we're doing ministry in the first place. I was one of those ministers and I've never forgotten the wisdom shared by a pastor with a pastor's heart. So I've tried to balance my worship and connection to God with the tasks of ministry like preaching, teaching, visiting members, and holding meetings.

    The words Bishop Simpson shared with me need to be heard today now more than ever because I fear many are so caught up in the doing of ministry that they have forgotten the Lord of the work. They have forgotten or got away from their worship of God. It is evident by this trend of celebrity preachers who sit in sanctuaries across the country and receive adoration and respect from the people of God, while not worshipping and honoring the one who first called them to the seat. This trend is so widespread because they have lost a sense of who they are before God and their churches are partly responsible for supporting this culture of idolatry and misplaced worship. Preachers, you are not that important that you cannot worship God. Churches, stop calling pastors to lead you who do not worship God and I am not talking about the exhortations to praise they give when the microphone is in their hand. They should worship well before it is time for them to preach. I know it sounds old fashion but churches ought to expect their pastor to come out of the office and join the rest of the people of God in the sanctuary as they worship the One who is worthy of adoration and glory.

      Some preachers may argue that such a practice is a part of their church tradition, particularly those in mainline church traditions where there is not a lot of standing, moving around, and spontaneous worship. In these churches there may be an expectation that the minister remain seated, is calm, and has a serious tone about him or her. It may be a part of the history and practice of particular black churches but I would argue it is a practice that needs to be amended. Preachers should be active worshippers. Preachers should exercise leadership by example in worship. I believe this is closer to the teachings of the Bible than the practice of sitting and looking important. There is no doubt that I have a philosophical and theological difference with black churches in the mainline tradition. I believe the traditions of Pentecostalism served as a corrective to staid black churches that minimize the practices of the Spirit for the politics of cultural respectability, which is a contributing factor to the current congregational ethos of the Black Church. As a Pentecostal and Baptist minister, I have been formed by pastors who worship God and I thank God for the way they modeled before me and the church, how to be a minister who is responsive and open about worship. The tradition of the preacher as worshipper needs to be recovered and increase in influence in today's Black Church. We need more preachers who model humility and who worship God with the people he has called them to serve.

Preachers who worship God in their churches highlight the reality and importance of the spirituality that undergirds everything the church is about. Preachers like this can have a profound influence on how the congregation understands and participates in worship. While worship is the preacher's first ministry, teaching and modeling the principles of Scripture are pretty high on the list, even in the top five. A core part of ministry is teaching and preachers need to understand that one of the important truths or principles to teach their churches is how to worship. Preachers do this both in word and action. Teaching on the Psalms or about Temple worship are two examples that come to mind of teaching the importance and the elements of worship. The language of Psalms pervades black churches.

> *O sing unto the Lord a new song for he hath done marvelous things* (Ps 98:1).

> *Make a joyful noise unto the Lord all ye lands. Serve the Lord with gladness. Come before his presence with singing* (Ps 100:1-2).
>
> *Bless the Lord, O my soul, and all that is within me, bless his holy name. Bless the Lord, O my soul and forget not all his benefits* (Ps 103:1-2).
>
> *O give thanks unto the Lord; call upon his name; make known his deeds among the people* (Ps 105:1).
>
> *Praise ye the Lord, praise God in his sanctuary…praise him with the sound of the trumpet…praise him with the timbrel and dance…let everything that hath breath praise the Lord. Praise ye the Lord* (Ps 150:1, 3, 4, 6).

I have heard the Psalms in worship services in black churches my entire life. Scriptures like these are usually followed with some amens and shouts of joy to God. Black churches do an adequate job centralizing the call to worship and some expectation that we are supposed to worship God.

Some even highlight the various ways to worship: singing, dancing, and giving thanks. They do so largely because preachers have taught them to do this. This aspect of teaching worship continues in many churches. But the part that is missing is the preacher who teaches about worship through his or her actions. There is more to teaching on worship than just exhorting people to praise the Lord or to worship

God. The preacher teaches about worship by what they do in the worship space. It says a lot about how they see themselves and why worship is important in the first place. In other words, preachers need to do more than tell the church to praise the Lord, he or she needs to lead the church in worshipping God by example.

This is important because it will help to change the larger culture of the church. You might find this hard to believe but there are a lot of churches filled with people who do not know how to worship God. I've seen them. I've worshipped in many churches like this. I know it sounds strange but let me explain. There is a difference between holding a church service and having a service of worship. Some churches have been carrying on for so long and have had so much leadership transition and so many years of struggling to keep the church alive that they've forgotten how to worship God when they gather together.

It is bizarre to see people just sit and look for an hour and a half to two hours and then leave. There is little to no investment of spiritual energy in worship. They don't sing. They don't stand. They don't raise their hands. They don't pray. They sit and look at the worship leader and the preacher. For these people, this is worship. But that is not worship. There is not a single Psalm that exhorts people to respond to the Holy in such a way and please do not quote the Psalm that says, "Be still and know that I am God" (Ps 46:1). The Psalmists is not talking about that. At first, I thought people do this because they don't know God but the more I see this and think about it I believe it is largely because they don't know how to worship God.

I recommend three things that pastors can do to change the culture of our churches and to teach our people about worship. **First, it is essential for preachers to worship God with the people and before the people.** Preachers are not just in church to deliver the sermon. They are converted, forgiven, Spirit-filled Christians who have experienced God's amazing grace. As Christians, they gather on the first day of the week to worship God and lift up the name of Jesus the Christ along with other Christians. They may have titles and degrees. They may be gifted and eloquent speakers but they are first and foremost Christians, believers in the resurrected Son of God. This is critical and cannot be overstated or minimized. Centralizing one's Christian identity helps the preacher and the people to see themselves rightly as fellow believers, as sisters and brothers in Christ, and as the people of God. There is a commonality, a bond that inextricably ties preacher and people together.

It is important for preachers to see themselves as Christians, as fellow believers, because it guards them from becoming "just a professional minister" but rather a person with a deep and living faith. It is a common temptation for preachers to fall into the trap of thinking they are "only" preachers. In restaurants and stores when members or people who know them see them they often refer to them as the preacher or my preacher. This title can almost completely absorb or take over one's identity. These men and women are called preacher all the time, so much so that a lot of members may not even know their preacher's birth name. Sadly, some love the title preacher more than their own name. The danger is that this models a primarily functional faith. To some preachers, faith is primarily for the tasks of ministry and is not a core part of their being or Christian identity. "I do this for the people." "It is for them."

Comments like this come from ministers who have disassociated themselves from the people they're called to serve. They no longer identify themselves with the people but rather as outsiders, separate from the body of believers they serve. They are performers, doers of the main task in a church service, which is preaching. Such beliefs are problematic on many levels and contribute to preachers not worshipping with the people. Instead of a functional faith, preachers need a living faith. In other words, what they do as preachers springs from who they are as Christians. They are men and women living out their faith and serving God as ministers. They are not just pulpiteers and public religious performers. They preach out of the wellspring of an experience with God, a connection to God, and messages they receive from God.

Second, it is important to worship God before the preaching moment. I say this because I believe that preaching is ultimately an act of worship and not something performed for the people of God. This may be my biggest critique of some preachers. They do not worship God before the preaching moment and I believe it contaminates the atmosphere of reverence for God and sets a bad example for other preachers. It always saddens me to see how many preachers carry on in church today. They enter the sanctuary and take their seat with their "spiritual" and "dignified" demeanor. Like the Pharisees and scribes, they love the "chief seats" in the church and soak up the ambiance that belongs God. They sit there and try their best to look important. Many don't sing songs along with the people of God. They don't get out of their seat. They refuse to raise their hands to God or bow before Him. They sit. Then when it is preaching time, they want the people gathered at church to do the very thing they did not do throughout the service, which is to worship God. I always found that to be ironic. I have often wondered to myself why the people should praise God now that you are in front of them.

Contemporary preaching desperately needs a shift in order to recapture its relevance for a society that is plummeting into atheism and nominalism. The church does not need performers but preachers who worship the God they claim to speak for and to do so with the people they are called to serve and lead. Worshipping before the sermon means that the preaching moment is a part of the preacher's worship and service of God and is openly offered before the people of God. This is a fundamentally different orientation for preachers than the celebrity model that is destroying the spirit of the faith.

Worshipping before the sermon also models who the real "wonder" is in the preaching moment. It is God and not the preacher. Their education and skills are not the reason for wonder in worship. It is God's hand on them and God's voice in them. God speaks to his people through the preacher instead of "pastor preached a word." This shift can greatly strengthen modern preaching.

Third, it is important that the preacher refuses to accept worship or veneration. Preachers must guard themselves from idolatry of self and they cannot let the people they serve fall into idolatry by worshipping and giving glory to them. They cannot allow any confusion in their church about their significance and place in God's order. God does not share his glory with the men and women he calls to ministry. Ministers must always be on guard against the temptation to idolize themselves or other preachers. The first two commandments in the Decalogue warn against idolatry.

> *Thou shalt have no other gods before me. Thou shalt not make unto thee any graven image or any likeness of anything that is in heaven above or that is in the earth beneath…thou shalt not bow down thyself to them, nor serve them: for I the Lord thy God am a jealous God* (Ex 20:3-5).

Throughout the Old Testament, we read about God's strong condemnation of idolatry. It was a sin he punished Israel for severely, sending them into exile. It serves as a warning to all Christians, particularly those who are called to represent the Holy One. As preachers, we dare not allow ourselves to become cultural and congregational idols, distracting people from their focus on God. One way to discourage this practice is for preachers to encourage their congregations to see them as fellow believers. But the strongest way to discourage the idolatrous worship of preachers is for you to worship God. Show the people you know who is above you and who is worthy of worship. It is partly the responsibility of preachers to make sure they do not allow themselves to be worshipped. If they perceive they are being lifted up or treated like a golden calf, they must quickly reject this in practical ways by coming out of the office a little earlier, getting up out of their seat during worship, singing along with the congregation or choir, raising their hands to God, verbalizing praises to God, and maybe even praising God in the holy dance.

The holy dance, commonly called shouting in black churches, is both a spontaneous expression of joy and a public display of ecstatic and reckless love for God. To shout is to be filled with such love for God that it can only be expressed bodily as one dances to the rhythms of the Spirit and drum beat of heaven. Such joy and ecstasy that people display in football stadiums, other sports arenas, and musical concerts rightly belongs to God. Who better to lead churches in radical worship than preachers? Nothing discourages and breaks the spirit of idolatry like worship. These three things help the congregation recognize that preaching is an act of worship, not a form of entertainment and that their focus needs to be centered on God and not necessarily how he is using the preacher.

Sing a Hymn or Pray

When the preacher gets up to preach there is a certain level of anticipation in the church. There is even excitement during times of high praise if the choir sings an inspiring and moving song. People are praising God. Some are even crying. Many are opening their hearts to God. Vulnerability abounds. This is a sacred moment for the preacher. We can stand before the people in these moments and take advantage of the people, drawing attention to ourselves as if we are the solution to their problems. Or we can be messengers of God. The pre-sermonic hymn was one way to center the congregation on God. It was a way to ground the preacher in preparation for the word that God had given him or her to deliver. That is why I will lift up my voice on occasion and sing a song before I preach because I've learned the real value of this. I am not a gifted or capable singer.

The Bible describes my singing as "a joyful noise" in Psalms 100. I fear that my singing will only draw attention to myself because it is so bad. I don't want to draw attention to myself and I definitely do not want to embarrass myself. I am sure there are a few other preachers who know what I am talking about. They couldn't carry a note in a ten-gallon bucket. They may not be able to sing but the principle of the pre-sermonic hymn can be applied in other ways. So what I've learned to do is to pray before my sermon and use the prayer in a similar way as the pre-sermonic hymn. I use scriptures from the Psalms and appropriate pauses with closed eyes to get myself grounded and to remind the church that this is the moment we expect to hear a message from God, not from me. This can be an effective approach. Another solution is for the preacher to worship God during the selection before they preach. Preachers can use this song in a consecratory way. They can mediate, pray, raise their hands, and or sing along with the choir. This is another way to model the importance of worship and guards against treating the preaching moment like a form of entertainment or a performance.

You should pay attention to what people say when they leave a worship service. Pastor preached a word! He or she tore it up! He wrecked it! She killed the house! He or she did the thing! These colloquial expressions, prominent among black clergy, are fun and well-meaning attempts to compliment the preacher for delivering a good and powerful sermon. I hear them all the time and agree many times with their assessment. Black preachers can be gifted by God in unique ways! We should, however, pay attention to them because though well intended, they reveal something about the psyche of people and what resonates with them after the preaching moment ends. There is a tendency in Black churches to focus on the preacher and to give the preacher credit or "the glory" for the good that people experienced in the preaching moment.

Conclusion

Preachers need to be reminded of the story of David. He was a young man when Samuel came to his house and anointed him as the next king of Israel. His job at that time was a shepherd. Years later

God blessed him. He reached the pinnacle. But it wasn't enough. Instead of acknowledging God for all that he was blessed accomplish, he took things that did not belong to him. He raped Bathsheba and had her husband Uriah killed. He then took Bathsheba to be his wife. These tragic events opened up David's life to years of turmoil, strife, and violence in his own family. Even his son Solomon fell because he couldn't handle the blessings God bestowed on him and the kingdom was divided. This story is apropos for preachers. God blesses us richly and entrusts a lot of things into our hands, namely the calling to preach the immeasurable riches of the gospel. Besides the knowledge of God and salvation, there is no greater blessing than the calling to preach. The question is, "Can we handle God's blessing to preach?"

      In today's world of celebrity preachers, the culture of preaching has changed. Like David on the rooftop contemplating taking Bathsheba for himself, too many preachers have forgotten what got them there in the first place. In all their success, they forgot it was their faith in God's promises and love of God that set them on the path to ministry. It was not their ability. It was their willingness to say yes to God. Years later, they sit in the trappings of success and beautiful sanctuaries; seduced by the blessings that accompany the calling. Preaching has become a show, a performance in rhetoric, human wisdom, and charisma instead of a demonstration of the power of God. The people get worked up and love you. There are endless invitations to preach in other churches. But under it all is a man or woman with a dying spirit because they are not connected to God. They are merely professional ministers.

After David's fall, he returned to some of things that he did before he became a high king. He turned back to God. Psalm 51 provides some insight into this turn and I recommend reading it because I believe preachers need it today. We need a return to worship. We need to see ourselves in the proper light- as men and women called by God and in submission to him. I hope to see more preachers drawing on the resources of worship before preaching so as to help both themselves and the people understand that this is about God and not us.

Chapter Five

Dealing with Opposition and Disillusionment in Ministry

With hope in his heart and excitement pulsating through his body, the young man accepts a call to pastor a small country church. He is eager to begin and expects God to change lives, save souls, strengthen churches, encourage the weak and meet needs. Through preaching and teaching the word of God, the young pastor knows that God is going to do great things. After five years, the young pastor is on the brink of leaving the ministry altogether. For years he has convened over contentious church meetings.

Some church members have resisted and fought almost every idea and plan he sought to implement. He has witnessed deep divisions that tear at the fabric of a congregation, divisions that are rarely healed. There are people who don't like each other and refuse to work together. Arguments over the color of carpet and who is picking up the trash in the parking lot have quenched the fire and excitement that he felt what seems like decades ago. Feeling disappointed, distraught and disillusioned, the young pastor plans to announce his resignation from the church and plans to leave the ministry for good.[12] What happened?

Again, sadly, this fictional narrative is being played out all across the country. Statistics on clergy health tell us that there are a growing number of pastors leaving the ministry in alarming numbers. According to some clergy surveys, 33% felt burned out within their first five years of ministry while 40% of pastors and 47% of spouses are suffering from burnout, frantic schedules, and/or unrealistic expectations.[13] One of the reasons they are doing this is because of the unexpected opposition and disillusionment with the rigors and difficulties of ministry.

Opposition and Disillusionment in Ministry

No one goes into ministry expecting opposition or worse yet, rejection, but both are a part of ministry. No one wants to be the preacher with a message that many do not take the time to heed or worse yet they don't even take seriously. You preach sermons on unconditional and universal love of all people yet you see people love only those who agree with them or look like them. You preach sermons on the importance of prayer and a personal relationship with God yet many in the church are not interested. They only pray when

---

[12] Some pastors are committing suicide because of years of opposition and disillusionment. I recommend reading my study of clergy suicide entitled *Dying to Lead* (Seymour Press, 2015).

[13] Ibid., 61-63.

asked in church or when they need something from God. You preach sermons on doing ministry in the community and meeting others needs and watch only a few committed members listen and participate in ministry while the rest only look to their own affairs. You just don't expect unbelief and disobedience to the gospel to be so widespread in a congregation of people who profess to love God and follow Jesus Christ. Maybe that is the problem. We don't really prepare preachers for the realities of ministry.

What I've Seen Ministry Colleagues Face

When I started out in ministry, I had no idea what ministers face. I naively thought that the church is a place of love and compassion because it is filled with mostly Christians who are saved and filled with the Spirit. Years later, I have seen the underside of ministry. It is mean, ugly, dirty, hateful, and destructive. I have seen pastors dismissed from churches for no reason other than the power brokers no longer wanted them. I have seen pastors slandered and falsely accused of wrong-doing and misconduct which caused confusion in their churches, communities, and families. I have seen pastors threatened by cowardly notes put on the window of their cars and slid under the doors to their study. I have seen spouses, many who became former spouses, leave pastors because they no longer want to do ministry. I have seen colleagues kicked out of churches because they have educational credentials and now the church does not want them. I have seen colleagues humiliated by congregants who would interrupt sermons with rude comments and insults. I have seen colleagues challenged to fights in the church. I have seen people befriend pastors for the purpose of gaining trust and later betraying that trust. I have seen spouses and children suffer from loneliness and neglect because ministry demands consume the pastor. I have seen pastors in bankruptcy because the church will not pay them a living wage. I wonder how my ministry would have changed had someone sat me down and told me about both the upside and downside of ministry. This has to be the way churches train and prepare men and women for the preaching ministry instead of allowing their naiveté to wither over the years as they confront the cold realities of church ministry.

    In Matthew 10, when Jesus commissioned disciples to go proclaim the good news of the kingdom of heaven, he prepared them for opposition and rejection. Jesus told them to "go" with the message but instructed them so they knew what to expect. He told them where to go preach and where not to go. He told them what to preach. He told them to do great works like heal the sick. He told them not to take additional clothing but rather to take only what they needed because their needs would be provided for by the people he was sending them to. And Jesus told them what to do about those who would not hear them. He said they should shake the dust off their feet and move on. He also prepared them for the persecution they would face, including beatings in the synagogues and divisions among families. Jesus told his disciples that they would be hated because of him but that they needed to endure. He concluded his instructions by reminding them that the disciple is not above his master. Jesus said if they call me Beelzebub how much more will they call you. In other words, if they treat me like a false teacher, they'll treat you like one too. In the face of this Jesus says do not be afraid. The implication here is not to waiver in taking the message because of persecution and challenges.

In the same way Jesus prepared his disciples for opposition and rejection, we need to prepare preachers, especially younger preachers, for what they will face in ministry. This is the part of ministry that few will talk about but many experience. Bible College and Seminary professors don't want to scare people off so they paint a picture of ministry that is unrealistic. Too many enter ministry ill equipped and unprepared for ministry's toll. We breed future candidates for burnout, depression, and suicide because they're unprepared. We have to prepare them for both opposition in ministry and the refusal of some to listen to them.[14] Preachers can spend years learning Hebrew and Greek, how to exegete a text, and how to preach a biblically and theologically sound sermon but in the end it may fall on deaf ears. The Spirit may be speaking in your sermon but people may not have ears to hear. The temptation will be to take it personally. I caution you not to do that. At its core, it is a rejection not of you but rejecting the one who sent you. This is why it is so important to underscore the spiritual

---

[14] Part of dealing with opposition and disillusionment is determining if one is struggling with depression. Archibald Hart, *Coping with Depression in the Ministry and Other Helping Professions* (Waco: Word Books, 1984) provides a helpful study of depression in ministry.

dimension behind preaching and the spiritual dimension behind hearing and receiving the message.

Preaching is spiritual work. We are neither salesman nor performers. We are not selling merchandise. We are not performing for the audience's approval. We are preachers of good news and bearers of a message the world hates: love God, love your neighbor, do justice, be generous, forgive those who wrong you, live a holy life, and deny yourself. The gospel is for everyone but you are not called to reach everyone. You can reach some, maybe many, but not all. Some will not listen to your message. And some may persecute and speak all manner of evil against you for the message you bear.

Whether or not a person hears and obeys the gospel or refuses to hear and disobeys the gospel is a primarily spiritual issue. The preacher will need spiritual disciplines like prayer and a right attitude to handle this aspect of the preaching ministry. Praying to God about the frustrations that can potentially mount in your spirit is essential. Prayer provides release and perspective on ministry, especially when your prayer life is true communion with God. If this aspect of ministry is not handled rightly, it can crush the spirit of the preacher or make him or her bitter and defiant toward the people and the ministry itself.[15] There are two truths that should frame and ground the preacher's understanding of ministry.

---

[15] Pastors deal with grief in ministry. One thing that can help pastors deal with this aspect of ministry is reading on the effects of grief and ways to cope with it. Kenneth R. Mitchell and Herbert Anderson, *All Our Losses All Our Griefs* (Philadelphia: Westminster Press, 1993).

Some People Can't See the Light

The first truth is "some people cannot see the light." Many of us have encountered this in ministry. It is undoubtedly the most heartbreaking moment in preaching and evangelism. The glorious light of the gospel is shining right in front of them but they can't see it. Paul talked about this same thing in his second letter to the Corinthians.

> *If our gospel be hid, it is hid to them that are perishing in who the god of this world hath blinded their minds lest the light of the glorious gospel should shine* (2 Cor 4:34).

This is very helpful text. It sheds invaluable light on why some people do not hear and believe and obey the gospel. Paul describes these people as lost. They are lost because the god of this world has blinded their minds. Because they are blind, they do not believe. This text points to deeper spiritual issues that must ground the preacher and guide his or her ministry.

One of the reasons preachers struggle within themselves today over those who do not hear the message is that they've been influenced more by the philosophy of pragmatism than the teachings of the Bible. Pragmatism maintains that the truth of something rest in the fact that it yields results. If it works, then it is true. The degree of influence this philosophy has on how we do ministry today would surprise you. Everybody wants results. And we want results as quickly and efficiently as possible. The worst part of this philosophy is that it has no way of accounting for why something does not work or bring results besides assigning blame. We operate with the assumption that if one is effective it will yield results.

In other words, if it doesn't work something must be wrong with you or the method you are employing. This is one reason why pastors and church leaders run from conference to conference learning new techniques to improve their preaching and enhance their ministries. While it is commendable that pastors want to nurture and cultivate their gifts, I believe we need to challenge the culture of pragmatism and reject the idea that the right technique or method will make us effective. God did not call us to be pragmatic pastors. God called us to be faithful pastors. Results in ministry is a complex matter with much beyond our control. We can acquire and nurture our preaching skills to maximize the possibility of reaching people with the good news but we cannot guarantee results.

Balancing the Toll and the Rewards of Ministry

Second, ministry is spiritually demanding. Ministry takes a toll. Giving oneself for the sake of the advancement of the gospel is not an easy task. In fact, it is very demanding. The prophets and apostles of God in the Old and New Testament can attest to the incredible challenges of ministry. Even Jesus experienced challenges during his earthly ministry. Religious leaders, political officials, and the people questioned Jesus about his teachings, ministry methods, and his authenticity. His professional peers were incredibly hard on him.

Those close to Jesus misunderstood him. People had selfish and less than honorable expectations of him. The crowds were mostly interested in what they could get from Jesus. Was Jesus their messiah? The one who would deliver them from Rome? Jesus was denied by one of his close disciples and betrayed by another. He was executed on the cross at the recommendation of the very crowds of people who celebrated him just a week earlier.

Paul can attest to the toll of ministry. He had it about as bad as any of us dealing with churches in Asia Minor. In 2 Corinthians 11:16-33, Paul talked about his own suffering in ministry. He was imprisoned. Beaten with 40 stripes by fellow Jews five times. Beaten with a rod. Stoned three times. Ship wrecked. Surrounded by perils while traveling. Confessed to being weary, in pain, hungry and thirsty, cold and naked, and burdened with the concerns of the churches. The work of preaching and ministry is one challenge after another, which is why Paul compares ministry to running a race (1 Cor 9:16-27). Some experience disillusionment because of the continual and unrelenting challenges. Some preachers just get worn down.

This can all sound like a lot of bad news- I can preach but people cannot see the glorious light of the gospel. I can expect a life of continual challenges and battles as a minister. This is not bad news. It is a sobering dose of reality. More ministers need to enter ministry understanding the nature of this sacred work. But that is not all there is to the work of ministry. There are many rewards. When I say rewards, the tendency is to think of heaven but I am not talking rewards in heaven.

There are many rewards of doing ministry. Let me name just a few. One of the greatest rewards is being a part of the conversion of a sinner. It does not matter if you were witnessing to them individually or if they heard a sermon and decided to turn to God, having some part of this wonderful act is very rewarding. You cannot imagine the eternal impact of turning one sinner to God. Another reward is helping people understand the Bible and their faith in a deeper way. It is a privilege to teach people the truths of Scripture and the ways of God. Romans 12:2 connects transformation to the renewing of the mind. In other words, Christians experience transformation to the extent their minds understand and apply the truths of God. When we preach and teach, we work as agents of the Spirit to bring about transformation in the lives of God's people.

One reward that I particularly love is fellowship with the saints. Fellowship is one of the great blessings of ministry. Whether at a get together in the basement of an older church or at a state of the art dining hall in a newly constructed church, sitting around the table with the saints and breaking bread is a true joy and foretaste of heaven. The last reward I will mention may sound strange but it is not. It is very rewarding to sit with people in the hard places in life- in sickness, amidst crisis, and during times of bereavement. For me, this is one of the most sacred aspects of the call to the preaching ministry. Preachers are given access into people's lives during difficult times. We sit at bedsides, in homes, at graveyards, and church altars as people face their mortality, deal with loss, and look to God for guidance and comfort. During these moments, we don't have to have all the answers. We only have to be there and give witness to the deep love God has for the world. Ministry is very rewarding. I could write for days on this.

It is important to lift up the rewards of doing ministry because ministry can be so demanding. Being reminded of the rewards of ministry balances the toll of ministry. And balance is essential if you want longevity in ministry. In addition to bringing balance, an awareness of the rewards reminds you of two things: why you do ministry in the first place and that ministry makes a difference. No matter how long you hope to work as a minister, it is critical to never forget why you answered the call in the first place; to make a difference in the world for the gospel of Christ. Without it, your ministry can end with burnout, misconduct, or suicide because you get lost and become hopeless and disillusioned in the midst of opposition and challenge.

Conclusion

I want to offer some very practical guidance to negotiating this aspect of ministry.

1. Self-care is very important. Pastors must learn to take care of themselves. Exercise and proper diet are both expressions of

self-care. Taking vacations and days off are additional ways to care for oneself. Getting sleep is also necessary.

2. Feed your spirit and continue to cultivate your relationship with God. Do not allow ministry to replace it. Spiritual disciplines like prayer, meditation, fasting, retreats, and journaling will feed your spirit. Listen to sermons to feed your spirit, not to duplicate for next Sunday's message.

3. Do not take your frustration out on the people you are called to serve. Do not give in to the temptation to abuse congregants in the preaching moment. Do not use your sermon as an occasion to address personal issues and vendettas. When dealing with mounting frustration, schedule an appointment with a therapist to ascertain whether there are mental health challenges that are fueling your frustration. You may also want to consult a ministry supervisor or trusted colleague to discuss your frustration and explore ways to cope with it.

4. Be less willing to take credit when God uses you to bless others. When they hear the word of the Lord with joy and gratitude, do not take credit for it. Humbly tell them "thank you" but give the glory to God who made it all possible. Be very careful how you manage success in ministry. The temptation will be to accept the credit for what God does through you and around you. Giving God the glory frees you

from the reverse effect of when you are not heard or when "success" as fickle people envision does not happen. When things do not work out, don't blame yourself. You are a part of a much larger plan that God has for the world.

5. Remember that you are not alone. You share the challenges and rewards of ministry with others who are a part of the company of heaven and many contemporaries who pastor large and small churches around the world. We all have experienced rejection and opposition and have at times wrestled with disillusionment in ministry. We are all in this together. We are not competing against one another. We are all on the same team. So reach out to a colleague and offer support.

6. Do not ever forget that you are making a difference. You may not always be able to measure it but you are making a difference. One of my favorite scriptures is Galatians 6:9 that says, "So let us not grow weary in doing what is right, for we will reap at harvest time, if we do not give up." It is human to grow weary in ministry. What keeps us going is the reminder that our work makes a difference. The promise in the second clause reminds that "in due season" we shall reap. Due season is not only harvest language it is also eschatological language. It means that our good works are an intricate part of God's eternal plan. Your good really matters. Now you may not understand

how your good fits into God's providential plan but that shouldn't stop you from doing good anyway. But you should know that good reverberates both in time and eternity. God is not mocked. There will be a time for reaping both in this life and the next.

Chapter Six

Bishops and the Black Church:
New Boundaries in Black Church Spirituality and Polity

Last year, a friend of mine shared a link on his Facebook page. The link led to an interesting interview discussing the popular trend of bishops in an increasing number of black churches. I clicked the link and watched an episode of the *Lexi Show,* provocatively titled *Illegitimate Bishops.* As the show began, the host expressed her amazement at the number of people who call themselves 'bishop' and 'doctor' without going through the proper channels. In other words, some pastors become bishops without credible educational training and outside the guidelines of an ecclesial structure for who can become a bishop, how one can become a bishop, and when one can become a bishop. To demonstrate this, she went online and found an organization to give an ordination certificate and credentials as a bishop. In order to get to the bottom of this, she interviewed three bishops: Paul Morton, Jerry Hutchins, and Lester Love.

These men are ordained bishops in the Full Gospel Baptist Fellowship, a fellowship of churches that originated in 1994 among African American Baptist churches that adopted charismatic spirituality and an Episcopal structure. These bishops discussed the trend among pastors who are becoming bishops and discussed the irony of how many of these pastors have had unsuccessful ministries. Bishop Morton asked, "How can these questionably appointed bishops lead other pastors?" *Lexi* exposed the startling lack of educational and ecclesial standards governing the ordination, appointment, and consecration of bishops. The panel of bishops discussed the standards to which Full Gospel Fellowship Baptist bishops are held. They seemed to suggest that this should be standard in more ecclesial circles.

    Needless to say, this video generated a good amount of comments on my friend's Facebook page that day. For me, it also raised a host of questions that have since been on my mind. Lexi and many other influential figures have begun to take note of what has become a growing trend and significant development in African-American churches today. Martha Simmons, president and publisher of the *African-American Pulpit*, mentioned the rise in the use of titles as one of the 21 trends in the Black Church.[16] It seems that more pastors value and want important titles like 'bishop' and 'doctor.' Bishops in black churches are not new. What is new and significant are the increasing number of church leaders who call themselves bishops and the congregational and organizational reconfigurations that this has brought about. For example, there are an increasing number of Baptist pastors who are forming fellowships among other Baptist Churches or connecting with nondenominational or Pentecostal

---

[16] Martha Simmons, "Trends in the African American Church," *African American Pulpit*: Vol 10 No. 2 (Spring 2007), 15.

churches and becoming bishops. This is a trend worthy of further exploration.

African-American bishops are not new. They have been around since the 1800s. Richard Allen became the first presiding bishop in the African Methodist Episcopal (AME) Church in 1816 and later Daniel Alexander Payne was consecrated as bishop in 1852. James Varick was ordained bishop of the African Methodist Episcopal Zion Church in 1822. William Henry Miles and Richard Vanderhost were the first bishops in the Colored Methodist Episcopal (CME) Church in 1870. In the early part of the twentieth century, Charles H. Mason became the presiding bishop of the Church of God in Christ, Charles Price Jones presided as bishop over the Church of Christ (Holiness) and Garfield Haywood was bishop of the Pentecostal Assemblies of the World. Ida Robinson, a bishop in the Mt. Sinai Holy Church, was an exception to what was an early norm among African American churches, that only men could be bishops.

Today, some African-American denominations have made small steps toward including women in the bishopric with capable leaders such as Vashti McKenzie in the AME Church and Teresa Snorton in the CME Church while others like the Church of God in Christ do not ordain women as bishops or even as pastors.

As you can see, these people are all bishops in churches with an Episcopal structure, meaning churches governed by select individuals called 'bishops.' Bishops preside over churches in jurisdictions, regions, or districts within a single state and sometimes preside over churches in multiple states. From a historical standpoint, the episcopacy in the contemporary Black Church is linked to the large number of African Americans in the Methodist churches since the early nineteenth century, which later gave rise to Holiness, Pentecostal, and nondenominational churches in the twentieth and twenty-first centuries, all of which have bishops. Becoming a bishop takes time in these churches. It requires one to begin as a local pastor and advance to positions such as ruling elder or district supervisor spending years overseeing pastors and congregations while working with a presiding bishop. At that point, one is appointed or elected as a bishop, a qualitatively different process than the one adopted by some African American churches.

So, what is the big deal? What is causing so much controversy and debate? Two things are happening. First, there are an increasing number of bishops in churches that have not historically been governed by bishops. This is particularly true in African-American Baptist churches, which typically have a congregational polity. The Full Gospel Baptist Fellowship, for example, is a clear deviation from congregational governance. Paul Morton formerly served as the presiding bishop of a fellowship of Baptist churches that have adopted an Episcopal structure. Today Bishop Joseph Walker III serves as the presiding bishop of the Full Gospel Baptist Fellowship. Furthermore, there are an increasing number of bishops in the National Baptist Convention. This trend is causing quite a stir as more traditional

Baptist pastors question the validity of the office of bishop in the Baptist Church.

Second, there are an increasing number of predominantly African-American nondenominational churches. These churches are not affiliated with historic black denominations like the AME Church, CME Church, National Baptist Convention, the Church of God in Christ, or the Pentecostal Assemblies of the World. Yet they have adopted the Episcopal structure. Among these nondenominational churches, many pastors call themselves bishops. What is particularly ironic about this practice is that many of these bishops do not exercise oversight of a jurisdiction, region, or district of churches with a host of pastors to oversee. They are mostly pastors of a single congregation and in some cases may participate in a fellowship of non-denominational churches.

There are bishops who serve as pastors of churches with membership as large as ten thousand to memberships of 10 or 20 people. This too, has caused a quite a stir. And so I ask the following questions. First, what caused this shift within historic denominations and the emergence of non-denominationalism among African-American churches? Second, why has the episcopacy become so popular? Is it the love of an honorific title or is it a signal of important issues emerging in African-American churches.

So What's in a Title?

There is no doubt that there are an increasing number of bishops in African American churches, even among churches with no ties to denominations with an Episcopal polity. There are also churches that historically had a congregational polity, who now have adopted facets of the episcopacy. Many are wondering why. A common answer given or one way to narrate this trend is to conclude that these men and women are glory-seeking leaders who love this honorific title. Simply stated, "They love the title 'bishop.'" While I am sure this is true of some leaders, I believe that it is a gross oversimplification. There is more to the emergence of the episcopacy in the Black Church than opportunistic leaders who love to hear the prefix "bishop" before their last name.

Such simplistic answers are indicative of a tendency by too many people to over-simplify religious phenomena among African Americans. Significant and complex religious phenomena are often dumbed-down and minimized. And sadly, too many religious and ministry professionals accept anecdotal evidence and over-simplified analysis to explore the religious beliefs, values, practices, and institutions of African Americans. Trends and developments in the Black Church are not as simplistic as many assume. In the remainder of this chapter and in the next, I will explore some reasons why bishops have become so prominent today. This is not a development that happened overnight.

The Black Church Has Changed

The truth is the Black Church has been changing in dramatic ways over the past two decades.[17] One of the causes for much of this change is linked to the influence of the spirituality, theology, and polity of Pentecostalism. Elements from Pentecostalism have transformed the landscape of the Black Church in the area of worship, with emphasis on the varied gifts of Spirit, the importance of an "anointed" preacher-pastor, and the prevalence of bishops. Beginning in the late 70s, Pentecostalism made significant inroads into mainline black denominations such as the AME church and the National Baptist Convention. These traditions were historically antagonistic to some extent of Pentecostalism but over time became more accepting of certain aspects. Pastors and congregations that responded to and adapted aspects of Pentecostalism without leaving their respective denominations were known as Neo-Pentecostals or Charismatics. This is a very important development because the seeds of Pentecostalism will continue to grow and transform the traditional polity, theology, and liturgy of black denominational churches. The seeds of the episcopacy were planted when these churches blended aspects of Pentecostalism into their churches. This is what gave rise to movements such as the Full Gospel Baptist Church Fellowship.

---

[17] If you want to examine broader trends in the Black Church I recommend reading Robert Franklin, *Another Day's Journey* (Minneapolis: Fortress Press, 1997); Larry Mamiya, "River of Struggle, River of Freedom: Trends among black churches and Black Pastoral Leadership" *Pulpit and Pew*. (Durham N. C., 2006) and a chapter on the new Black Church in Shayne Lee's book *T. D. Jakes: America's New Preacher* (New York: 2005).

Furthermore, in the 80s, the growth of African-American Word of Faith churches and nondenominational churches, as well as the prominence of televangelism paved the way for new configurations of ministry. Different forms of church and ministry radically challenged traditional denominational structures, congregational-based preaching, and smaller family churches. These different models of ministry gained significant traction in African-American communities. Today more African Americans attend nondenominationally affiliated churches, mega-churches, and watch pastors on television or via the internet than they did in previous decades, while fewer African Americans are tied to traditional mainline denominations, many of which seem resistant to these changes.

Today, we are in the third decade of what some studies call the "new Black Church" and in this new church, leadership, worship, and polity have been reconfigured. The emergence of the episcopacy has become an important part of the new Black Church. I am not saying the "newer" is better but I am doing two things. First, as a historian, I am chronicling this development in the Black Church, so that we can better understand the phenomena of bishops.

As a religious scholar, I am also trying to ascertain what this development signifies and says. Beyond the criticisms of this development or those who support this trend, we need to give attention to some of the issues that inform it.

A Closer Look at Why There Are Bishops Today:

Our guiding question has been "Why is there a need for bishops in churches without an Episcopal structure or bishops in nondenominational churches?" It is apparent that the Black Church is changing, especially due to the influence of Pentecostalism. However, the increasing interest in the episcopacy and the increasing numbers of bishops in African American churches are not just because of the influence of Pentecostalism. The changes in worship style, spiritual practices, and church polity are only part of the story. There is a functional dimension missed by popular critiques of this trend. There are more bishops in black churches because of the increased demand for new or different bishops from African American congregants and clergy. The real question is "What is driving the demand?"

The increased demand for different or new bishops is an indication of something wrong in denominational churches with an Episcopal structure, like the Church of God in Christ (COGIC), Christian Methodist Episcopal (CME), or Pentecostal Assemblies of the World (PAW). I believe one major reason African American Christians are doing this is the abuses some pastors, ministers, and other church members have experienced by denominational bishops. These Episcopal denominational churches are structured in a way that requires pastors and churches, many of which are small, struggling churches, to pay reports (think money) to the bishop. In some of these churches, those monies are for the bishop to use at his or her discretion, many of whom choose to keep those monies for themselves and the larger churches they serve. I spent years in a denomination like this as a pastor. I witnessed firsthand the abuse of bishops over pastors and churches. A bishop would come into small churches and take as much money as he could and the monies given to the bishop rarely trickled back down to churches and pastors that may need them or local communities. In the cases when pastors and churches could not pay a report to the bishop they were embarrassed, often publicly. There is an incredible amount of pressure to not be the pastor or church that cannot make a report to the bishop. Possibly the worst aspect of this kind of relationship is if pastors needed counsel from the bishop, they found that bishops were unavailable and some bishops discouraged their pastors from contacting them. Experiences like these are very much a part of the demand for something different.

The Black Church, for the most part, has been an institution committed to serving the needs of a marginalized and oppressed people, not the maintenance of structures that exist to serve religious leaders. Today there is a clear disconnect with this system that offers few benefits for pastors and local communities. I am not surprise that there are a number of pastors, ministers, and congregants who leave these churches and find bishops and church structures where these practices are not replicated. Today, we see a number of pastors who are no longer willing to serve in churches with an oppressive tax system that does not benefit local churches or to follow bishops who are inaccessible to the pastors and ministers. Pastors in nondenominational churches and fellowships with bishops have access to them in ways pastors in denominational churches do not. This is an important factor in the emergence of the episcopacy in the new Black Church. Some of these bishops are not meeting the changing needs of African American churches and communities. In conclusion, I am not certain if the newer forms or structures of the episcopacy will meet these needs or if this trend is a signal of much deeper problems with Episcopal denominations. This will remain to be seen in the coming years.

One day a colleague of mine asked me if pastors and churches are dissatisfied with some of the practices, like paying reports to the bishop. "Why don't African American pastors and churches abandon the Episcopacy altogether?" I believe the answer is that the function and roles bishops play in the Black Church are too important to abandon. I want to explore the role of bishops in black churches and why it is important. This is the first issue that I will address.

The Scriptural Precedent for Bishops

The office of bishop has been in the church for almost two thousand years. Not only has it been in the church for all this time, it is attested to in the Bible. For these reasons, it is an office of great importance. African American churches generally take Scripture very seriously, and so, follow leadership models mentioned in texts such as 1 Corinthians 12: 27-28, 1 Timothy 3:1-7, and Ephesians 4:11. From texts like these, African American churches appoint pastors to teach and lead congregations. Bishops or overseers do these same functions and others that sometimes were fulfilled by apostles who appear to usurp pastors in authority and importance in the New Testament. For example, Paul was a prominent apostle in the New Testament who supervised churches in Corinth, Galatia, Thessalonica, Philippi, and pastors like Timothy and Titus.

This twofold model of a local congregational leader and a supervising leader of churches and pastors is very prominent in black churches. The only difference is that they appoint bishops to do the work previously done by apostles in New Testament times. In fact, I would maintain that the two major offices held by Black Church leaders are pastor and bishop, respected and sometimes revered offices in the Black Church. But the respect is not solely due to the fact that these offices are mentioned in Scripture. It has more to do with the function and work they take up in the church. Since people are aware of the work pastors do in congregations, I will not discuss it any further but rather focus on the work of bishops, which is a very illuminating feature of any study of this phenomenon.

The Functions of African American Bishops

What are some of the functions of bishops in African American churches? I will briefly mention three. First, bishops care for and oversee local and regional congregations. Sometimes they work with congregations across the nation. Bishops care for pastors and supervise their ministry activities. For example, in Methodist denominations, bishops place pastors in congregations and decide which pastor is an appropriate and good fit for a congregation and also when it is time to relocate a pastor to another congregation. They also handle the delicate and difficult issues that arise in churches when pastoral abuse and misconduct has occurred.[18] I know of one such bishop who had to go into a congregation where a pastor accidentally murdered his secretary (who was his lover) in the church office. It was an incredibly difficult situation for him to handle. Yet he did it with grace and strength. And today, that congregation is still going. This kind of work seems to go beyond the local responsibilities of a pastor.

Second, bishops serve as denominational and or organizational administrators. They facilitate programs and initiatives among the churches they oversee. They educate pastors, ministers, and church leaders. And they work as fund development officers who raise the necessary funds to support the work of the denomination and or organization, a portion of that going directly to them, which is why salaries for bishops are much higher than congregational pastors and why the office is so coveted by pastors and ministers.

Third, and in some cases, bishops serve as community leaders and even as national spokespersons on important issues affecting

---

[18] One area not often addressed in the debate over bishops are the ethics of episcopal and pastoral leadership in the Black Church. For example, bishops often make a biblical case for their leadership role. While this conversation is necessary, it is limited. Black Church leaders need to give deeper consideration to their understanding of authority as a religious leader and ethical ways to live that out in their churches, associations, and networks. The persistence of scandals and cases of misconduct are clear evidence that such conversations are long overdue. For those interested in exploring authority and ethics in ministerial leadership I commend Karen Lebacqz, *Professional Ethics* (Nashville: Abingdon Press, 1985) and Jackson Carroll, *As One with Authority* (Louisville: Westminster John Knox, 1991).

African Americans. For example, Bishop Henry M. Turner was a leader that addressed major issues affecting blacks and not just issues affecting his denomination. This function is not prominent today. Popular African American bishops are not outspoken leaders on important national issues like education, incarceration, healthcare, and unemployment. Most black bishops are also not theologians or religious scholars. In contrast to African bishops in the early church who were major theologians, African American bishops are rarely theologically trained and are not experts on doctrinal and or religious matters. Instead of serving as leading voices on social issues or theologians, many bishops spend an inordinate amount of their energy and time in church preaching sermons. Bishops are gifted preachers and are called upon to preach in local congregations and at a host of regional and national conferences, which have taken on a life of their own in black churches. It is rare to find an influential African American bishop who is not a gifted preacher and even rarer to find black churches who do not place a heavy demand on their preaching talents.

The Importance of Accessible Bishops

The episcopacy has been and continues to be reconfigured because these newer models are meeting needs in ways the traditional model is not. Pastors and leaders of various kinds are searching for an increased level of accountability, especially among independent, nondenominational churches, and mentoring (think leadership development). There is an increased level of scrutiny (think scandals) and heightened expectations placed upon clergy.

Churches expect them to produce results like the church down the street or the mega-church on television. As a result, more pastors are searching for mature and successful leaders, many of whom are bishops, to provide some structure and guidance for them and their ministries. Bishops are accessible and willing to lead pastors in navigating the tumultuous waters of modern ministry. As a result, church structures are changing as more pastors gravitate to bishops and organizations, many times while remaining within their traditional denomination. This is a part of why I believe the episcopacy is so prominent today. But there is so much more. I have provided a brief introduction to foster dialogue on this issue and hope that as the episcopacy continues to exercise incredible influence, this guide will encourage critical and creative thinking.

The Future of the Episcopacy

More than likely, pastors will continue to aspire to the office of bishop, and even will desire the title, when there is no office or structure accompanying it, for years to come. Bishops in African American churches will influence the shape of traditional and nontraditional churches. However, there are two looming problems that may undermine the episcopacy. There are signs of mistrust in bishops and much of it is linked to the issue of money or more accurately fundraising.

"Blessing the Bishop"

Many bishops expect and sometimes require other pastors and churches to pay them. They often use the language of "honoring the bishop" or sowing into your "prosperity connection" but its language that means one has to pay. What is so interesting about this trend is that it is carried out in non-denominational systems. These funds are not for denominational expenses. Instead the money goes directly to the bishop. It is possible that this system is or could be the same oppressive tax system used in African American denominations like the AME, CME, or COGIC churches. Instead of paying reports, these churches sow into their leader or kingdom connection and pastors and ministers are pressured to "bless" their bishop. Time will tell if pastors who left denominational churches because of the oppressive taxation system and lack of relationship with the bishop will find the same thing in nondenominational churches.

Bishops as Administrators and Preachers, not Theologians For the most part, bishops function as administrators and pastors of churches who oversee a network of churches and mentor other pastors. Many of the great bishops in today's Black Church fill this role. They work in denominations or a network of nondenominational churches. There are many reasons to commend this function of the bishopric. It is a good thing to have prominent bishops who pastor local congregations. It is a good thing that seasoned bishops lead denominations in appointing pastors to congregations and administering the affairs of a large network of churches. It is also a very good thing that bishops are available to mentor and lead other pastors.

However, I cannot help but hope that the future of episcopacy will see another role taken on by bishops. I hope that we see an emergence of bishops who are credible theologians and religious scholars. The Black Church needs bishops with Ph. D's from accredited institutions.

The Black Church needs bishops who are theologians and scholars who publish writings for the church. The truth is that many black scholars do not hold leadership positions in black churches and are not pastors. There is also a serious dearth of ecclesial leaders who are academically trained as theologians and scholars. Many bishops do not hold any theological degree. There are many without even a bachelor's degree. This practice should not continue because it means that the men and women who lead our denominations and networks of churches are not leading theological thinkers.

This current trend is in contrast to what happened in the early church. During the first five hundred years of Christendom, there was a long tradition of African bishops who were major theologians. Great thinkers and leaders such as Athanasius, Origen, and Augustine all led churches and influenced the broader church on theological issues. They wrote about the nature of Christ, how to interpret Scripture and how to understand sin just to name a few. This is the tradition that I hope becomes a part of the future of the episcopacy. Today, African

American bishops are not theologians. They are great preachers and leaders. But why can't they be great preachers and theologians?

For this to happen, many Black Church denominations and networks of churches will have to address this current anti-intellectualism. They will have to stop discouraging critical and creative thinking. They will have to give space in their programs and conferences for theologians and scholars to speak and exercise leadership. They will have to model respect for theologians and scholars in the same way they model respect for pulpit preachers and pastors. It will take some time before theologically trained leaders are not an oddity among black churches but it is absolutely essential if we are going to see bishops who can lead black churches as theologians and religious scholars.

Conclusion

These are exciting times in the Black Church. A lot is happening. A lot is changing. Some of it is for the better while some things seem to worsen the ways in which we are doing ministry in the church. Time will tell as leaders continue to emerge and push the envelope and redefine how we do church. I am sure that the episcopacy will be a part of the future of the church but have no idea what form it may take in the coming decade. That we will all witness together.

Chapter Seven

Pushing the Boundaries of Spirituality beyond the Four Walls of the Church

After one and a half decades into the 21st century, the Black Church stands at the crossroads between a renewed sense of spiritual and communal vitality on one hand and spiritual and social irrelevance on the other. African American pastors and congregations are making the choice either to equip their people with a faith that reflects a deep connection to God and a faith that changes the world or to equip people with a faith that is deeply connected to the evil workings of the world and a faith that is disengaged from the call to change the world to reflect the kingdom of God. In the next three decades, churches and their leaders will make decisions that will revitalize churches and communities or make decisions that will lessen the church's witness in communities. We stand at a significant crossroads that has implications for the church's relevance for decades to come. That is why I believe the greatest challenge to Black Church spirituality will be whether it finds expressions beyond the walls of its churches.

The Contemporary Crisis of Black Church Spirituality

Eddie Glaude's 2010 article entitled, "The Black Church is Dead" in the *Huffington Post* created a major debate between civic-minded leaders of the black community and religious leaders of black churches about the efficacy and existence of the Black Church.[19] Glaude bluntly stated that the Black Church is dead. What did he mean by this statement? His contention is that religion is important to African Americans but the idea that the Black Church is central to the religious lives of blacks has long been abandoned. There is data to back up Glaude's radical claim. For example, studies on attendance trends in American congregations show that the number of African Americans who no longer attend church are growing.

According to a recent survey of American religion, the number of African Americans who claimed they had no religion almost doubled from six percent to nine percent between 1990 and 2008. This, in addition, to declining number of African Americans who attend Methodist, Baptist, and other denominational churches are raising concerns that something is amiss in black communities nationwide.

Scores of black pastors across the nation took issue with his assessment of the death of the Black Church. They claimed that the Black Church is as viable today as it has ever been to the religious lives of black people. However, the debate over the supposed "death" of the Black Church has caused black pastors to miss the core issue he sought to raise. African Americans are choosing to practice their faith outside the bounds of the Black Church and this trend should serve as

---

[19] Eddie Glaude, "The Black Church Is Dead," *Huffington Post* (April 25, 2010).

a warning sign to pastors and ministry practitioners in the Black Church.

There are others who share Glaude's concern. Leaders such as Reginald Davis's text, *The Black Church: Relevant or Irrelevant in the 21st Century*, Robert Franklin's *Crisis in the Village: Restoring Hope in African American Communities*, and Stephanie Mitchem's *Name It Claim It: Prosperity Preaching in the Black Church* represent a growing chorus of voices, from both scholars and religious leaders, arguing that there is a serious decline in black churches. Without major reform, Black churches in the 21st century context, will slip further into irrelevance.

Reginald Davis grapples with the growing irrelevance of black churches. For him, the question of relevance is intricately tied to whether the Black Church will address the continuing suffering of black communities. Black Americans rank at the top in crime, murders, drug abuse, unemployment, incarceration, poverty, education, education deficiencies, and HIV/AIDS. Yet, so many in black churches are not addressing these issues in public venues and not involved in making substantive changes in these trends. Davis views the Black Church as a sleeping giant amidst a people in crisis and contends that the people in most black churches are "addicted to religiosity instead of liberation."[20]

---

[20] Reginald Davis, *The Black Church: Relevant or Irrelevant in the 21st Century* (Macon GA: Smyth & Helwys Publishing, 2010), 36.

Franklin and Mitchem believe that the growing popularity of the prosperity movement among African Americans is a sign that Black Church spirituality has turned to materialism and neglected commitments to justice and righteousness in the world. Franklin believes that the prosperity movement is "the single greatest threat to the historical legacy and core values of the contemporary Black Church tradition."[21] This alarming statement rests on his belief that this movement poses significant dangers to the spirituality and future of the Black Church.[22]

Four reasons are worth noting here. First, he argues that the movement's teachers tend to focus on institutional well-being at the expense of serving the vulnerable. Secondly, he claims that prosperity teachers deliberately suppress, ignore, and/or delete language about radical sacrifice for the sake of the kingdom. Thirdly, he suggests that the bishops and pastors of prosperity operate as spiritual entrepreneurs who know how to produce, package, market, and distribute user-friendly spirituality for the masses. Finally, and also somewhat connected to the aforementioned critique, the teachers rarely make stringent ethical demands because their primary concern is to market and distribute products. With leaders of the African American

---

[21] Robert Franklin, *Crisis in the Village: Restoring Hope in African American Communities* (Minneapolis: Fortress Press, 2007), 112.

[22] Franklin argues that the prosperity emphasis represents a shift of commitments away from love, service, and justice and resultantly poses not only a new threat for black clergy for a broader crisis of mission in the Black Church. It is in the context of this crisis of mission that Franklins offers such a strong rejection of black prosperity churches.

community on both sides of this issue it is necessary to identify what is at stake.

Mitchem frames her critique of the prosperity movement within the larger context of the black religious experience. Within the eclectic traditions of the Black Church, there is deep longing for something better. She says, "Longing has always been a significant component of black American spirituality. This longing signifies a story that is internal to black communities, the result of African American experiences within the context of the economy of the United States.[23] While longing for better, whether it is justice or economic progress, is not inherently wrong and understandable, the prosperity movement does not adequately reflect this deep tradition.

Among the many substantive critiques she offers, I will mention four. First, Mitchem states that prosperity preaching generally stresses the individual person's will over history as the God-approved route to overcoming racial oppression. In other words, the movement stresses the importance of the individual over community. Second, she suggests that a religion constructed for one's physical comfort ultimately does not assist spiritual maturity nor does a pushover deity represent a mature view of God.[24] Third, she claims that prosperity religions generally develop a theology of here and now. The leaders do not draw from centuries of theological development but the decades of

---

[23] Stephanie Mitchem, *Name it Claim it: Prosperity Preaching in the Black Church* (Cleveland: Pilgrim Press, 2007), 21.

[24] Ibid., 122.

their experience. Fourth, she critiques the meaning of faith in this brand of preaching. She says, "Faith cannot be reduced to simple platitudes, even if it is taken from a biblical passage but that it encompasses the belief, action, and trust of individual people and as person's in communities grow over a person's lifetime.[25]

Both Franklin and Mitchem have raised significant issues with this movement and what it represents for Black Church spirituality. It subverts the principle of liberation and justice by its failure to address systemic and structural inequality. It prioritizes individual attainment over communal and social responsibility. On a more fundamental level the movement fails to deal with structural inequalities and social issues, it fails to connect prosperity with the pressing social concerns of our community and rarely provides an agenda for social change or advancement but focuses on individual betterment. On a deeper level, it appears that this expression of teaching represents a troubling theological understanding of God. This is one reason why I argue that the Black Church stands at the crossroads between viability and anonymity.

Traditional Black Church, Insulation, Isolation

We need to understand the deeper causes of the current crisis among black churches in America because there are more problems than the varied expressions of prosperity teaching. Reginald Davis's assessment of the Black Church is helpful here. He claims the Black

---

[25] Ibid., 122.

Church is addicted to religiosity instead of liberation. In other words, African Americans preoccupy themselves with religious activity and neglect social ministry beyond the walls of the church. This statement identifies one of the major issues behind the crisis in spirituality that black churches are facing. Some black churches tend to isolate themselves from the communities they are called to serve. I believe some intentionally do this because they have little concern for their communities while others do this because of the way many African American churches function. In other words, they are not isolated from their communities due to a lack of concern. Rather, they are so preoccupied with church activities that they never really get around to doing work outside the walls of the church.

In order to adequately explore the issue of the Black Church's relevance in the 21st century, I must begin with two questions: "Is the Black Church out of touch and too dated to make a difference in the contemporary world" and if so, "How did the Black Church get out of touch with the world?" For eight years as a seminary administrator, I made numerous "site visits" to African American churches as a part of relationship building between the seminary and regional churches in West Virginia, Virginia, North Carolina, Ohio, Kentucky, Tennessee, and Maryland. In some respects, when I walked into some black churches, I immediately felt that I stepped back in time to the late seventies and eighties. Old school church is current in both cities and rural communities across the region. I later came to classify these churches as traditional. These churches employ the traditional model of Sunday school, 11 o'clock morning service, Sunday afternoon or evening service, Monday night choir practice, Tuesday night prayer service, Wednesday night Bible study or mid-week service, and Saturday fellowships of some kind or bake sales. In addition, weekly sermons admonish congregants with variations of old themes commonly heard in black sermons: "I've got a feeling that everything is going to be alright," "God is going to bless you," and "Keep on waiting on the Lord." While not all black churches can be characterized as traditional in this sense, there are a number of churches employing some aspects of this model of church ministry.

Traditional Black Church represents a model of church from an earlier time. I characterize traditional black churches in two ways. First, they are churches with *high activity and high expectations for participation.* Traditional church keeps members extremely busy attending church services, meetings, and functions to the extent that participation in the life of the church becomes a world unto itself. Second, they are churches with an *individualized and otherworldly spirituality.* Traditional Black Church places emphasis on individual piety. Get right with God. Live right. Pray more. Stay in the word. Don't miss church. Much of the preaching and worship centers on the congregants' personal relationship with God. In addition to this, there is considerable focus on spiritual and eternal matters. Pentecostal spirituality made significant inroads into the Black Church and because of this there is a lot of attention on the spirit world. "Spirit world" cosmology with its legions of angels and demons, strongholds, spiritual warfare, and contending with evil occupies the attention of parishioners. These matters are important to faith but the degree of attention given to what is other worldly is problematic.

My biggest critique of this model of church ministry is that it results in community isolationism. People are so busy with church that they don't have time to be the church in the world. Traditional black churches function as if church life is still the central aspect of life in the black community and requires attendance at most, if not all, church functions.[26] Many times this is done without due consideration of broader societal changes and how complicated this level of participation can be for families. Inevitably, with church members excessively busy with church services and activities as well as a spirituality that is individualistic and otherworldly, social withdrawal and social isolation occurs. Without leaders who intentionally model a vision of ministry and spirituality that both addresses the internal dynamics of congregational life and its external witness in society, black churches can slip into irrelevance. The traditional model of doing Black Church has become antiquated and ineffective in addressing the challenges of the contemporary world.

---

[26] On a deeper level, insulation and isolation are inevitable results of a church that serves as a safe space from structural oppression. The church has historically been a space and place of safety and community. Because of hostile social conditions linked to racism, African Americans have grown comfortable within the confines of sanctuaries and fellowship halls and developed sub-cultures that require modest to high levels of activity.

The Historic Debate over Spirituality in the Black Church

Critiques such as Glaude and Davis's are not new but are actually a part of the tradition of the Black Church, a tradition that has wrestled with the meaning and implications of church spirituality for work that goes beyond the walls of the church. In the book *Your Spirits Walk Beside Us*, Barbara Savage writes, "Throughout the twentieth century there were spirited debates among varied groups of African Americans about whether religious doctrines, religious people, and religious organizations were a blessing or a curse in the struggle for black freedom and racial progress."[27]

Prominent figures such as W.E.B. Dubois, Carter G. Woodson, and Benjamin Mays were critical of black churches role in addressing social issues and at different times called for a reformation of the Negro church. Their call for a reformation in the Black Church was fueled by what they perceived as a lack of concern for issues affecting black communities. Savage introduces contemporary leaders of the Black Church to this important historic debate and its bearing on the Civil Rights movement and how we understand black religion. Her work is important not only because it chronicles this history but also because of the ways it illumines the contemporary debate of the supposed death and irrelevance of African American churches.

---

[27] Barbara Savage, *Your Spirits Walk Beside Us* (Cambridge MA: Harvard University Press, 2008), 2.

The Black Church has held an important yet complex role in the political life of the African American community. On one hand, some leaders in black churches have been heavily involved in the political arena. For example, six black clergymen have been elected to Congress since 1970 while five more ran for Congress but were not elected. Two black clergymen have run for president. Black churches also figure prominently in encouraging voter registration and voter turnout. On the other hand, there has been a strong apolitical stance in the Black Church.

Many black pastors focus only on what they consider "spiritual" issues like salvation, prayer, and worship while neglecting to give attention to the role of the church and Christians in society. For this reason, parishioners in these churches ignore and do not involve themselves in political and social issues. These varying responses are not new. Debates over the political involvement of the Black Church go back to the Reconstruction period and were especially tense during the Civil Rights movement. The question before the modern Black Church will be the role its congregations take in the coming decades.

Conclusion: Toward a Social and Political Spirituality

What the Black Church needs is a spirituality that is both social and political.[28] I believe this is the model of spirituality modeled in the teachings of the Bible. There are three kinds of ministry in the Bible

---

[28] For a theological resource to undergird this approach to ministry I recommend Homer Ashby, Jr., *Our Home Is over Jordan* (St. Louis: Chalice Press, 2003).

that should inform the church's approach. In the Old Testament, the priests attended to matters of worship and the place of worship. Priests give great care to the worship of the Holy One. Both the Old Testament and New Testament talk about shepherds or pastors as those who provide care, teaching, and oversight for the people of God. Pastors are situated as local representatives of the larger care God has for his people.

Though mentioned in both testaments, the Old Testament prophet is a model of ministry that is critical for the institutional arm of religion and society in general. Prophets speak truth to powerful political, social, and religious leaders and use God's standard of justice to measure their institutions and actions in the world, especially their relation to the most vulnerable in society. Imagine if this threefold model of ministry became the norm among black churches.

What can revitalize black churches is a biblically-balanced approach to ministry that emphasizes the centrality of worship, ministry that cares for the needs of the people, and ministry that addresses matters of justice and righteousness in the world, especially among the institutions of the church. This priestly, pastoral, and prophetic model of ministry operates under the auspices of the Holy Spirit who gifts and anoints people to carry out this work. And it is important to make the connection between the Holy Spirit and ministry that touches priestly, pastoral, and prophetic issues.

Black churches should be priestly ministries that invite people to worship God openly and unashamedly and to be transformed by the presence of God. Black churches need pastoral ministries that enable people to experience a real relationship with the living Christ and ministries that preach and teach the Word of God with power, conviction, simplicity, depth, and honesty so that believers may truly live out their calling to give witness to the gospel of Jesus Christ. Black churches need prophetic ministries that address issues such as poverty, racism, sexism, militarism, etc. This model of ministry allows churches to attend to the spiritual, pastoral, and social needs of the people within and outside the congregation. I hope that more pastors and congregations employ this or other models of ministry that attend to the spiritual, pastoral, and social needs of their communities.

www.ingramcontent.com/pod-product-compliance
Lightning Source LLC
LaVergne TN
LVHW020932090426
835512LV00020B/3319

9 781938 373084